The Bible in Limerick Verse

Christopher Goodwins

To Michael & Myrtle,

With best wishes!

Christopher Goodwins
X

BOOKS

Winchester, U.K.
New York, U.S.A.

11 Feb '07

First published by O Books, 2006
An imprint of John Hunt Publishing Ltd., The Bothy,
Deershot Lodge, Park Lane, Ropley, Hants, SO24 0BE, UK
office@johnhunt-publishing.com
www.o-books.net

USA and Canada
NBN
custserv@nbnbooks.com
Tel: 1 800 462 6420 Fax: 1 800 338 4550

Australia
Brumby Books
sales@brumbybooks.com
Tel: 61 3 9761 5535 Fax: 61 3 9761 7095

Singapore
STP
davidbuckland@tlp.com.sg
Tel: 65 6276 Fax: 65 6276 7119

South Africa
Alternative Books
altbook@global.co.za
Tel: 27 011 792 7730 Fax: 27 011 972 7787

Text copyright Christopher Goodwins 2006

Design: Jim Weaver

ISBN-13: 978 1 905047 59 8
ISBN-10: 1 905047 59 2

A CIP catalogue record for this book is available from the
British Library.

Printed in the US by Maple Vail

Contents

Preface

The whole purpose of writing *The Bible in Limerick Verse* is to encourage people to *want* to read the Bible – *the real thing!*

The Bible in Limerick Verse came about as an evangelistic project, many years ago, when I translated the Parables of Jesus into limerick verse. I was originally planning to use these amongst the Epilogues that I had the privilege of presenting in the United Kingdom over a period of eighteen years, on *Westward Television,* and also on *Television South West.* They lay dormant however until 1999, when I undertook a personal Lenten challenge, to put the whole of the New Testament into limerick verse.

The subsequent publication in 2000 of *"The New Testament In Limerick Verse,"* was followed up in 2002 with the publication of *"The Old Testament And The Apocrypha In Limerick Verse."* It seems logical therefore in 2006 to combine the two books into one, as *"The Bible in Limerick Verse."*

Although originally classified under the genre of *"Humour,"* I always saw the work as a serious evangelistic attempt to encourage people to read their Bibles. As a former teacher, I knew full well how boring Religious Education had been at school – typically in the last period on a hot Friday afternoon, when pupils were tired and wanted to break off for the weekend. *How could we recapture their interest in the Bible?*

I feel therefore that *"The Bible in Limerick Verse"* is a way of reaching all sorts of people, who are crying out for something really different and interesting. It seems to have worked, judging by the feedback that I have received. University Professors and Bishops have written to say how exciting they found it. Prison Chaplains, and Clergy of all Christian denominations too, including Anglicans, Roman Catholics, Methodists, and Baptists. Children aged 7 and 9 saved up their pocket money to buy the books. One father wrote to say that it *"had rekindled the flame in his teenage son."* Grannies and granddads in their nineties, and young parents likewise, wrote to say how helpful this had been.

"It could start a revolution in the teaching of Religious Education" said one teacher. *"Just the thing for children to remember!"* said another. *"I thought it was the most inspirational and fun way of bringing the Bible to life!"* said a TV presenter. *"What a wonderful way of introducing people to the Bible!"* said a housewife. A Theological College Principal said that he *"would ensure that all his students would have a copy."*

Interest and publicity worldwide has been phenomenal, with requests for the work coming from Canada and the USA, Australia and New Zealand, South Africa, India, and all over the United Kingdom and Europe. In this sense, I am proud to have made an attempt to *"preach the Gospel in all lands,"* as Jesus commanded (in *Mark 16:15*). And as Jesus *(Luke 24:45)* *"opened their mind, that they might understand the scriptures,"* then I hope that this does the same.

I have tried to be faithful to the text, as well as highlighting the parts of my working-Bible that mean a lot to me personally. Hopefully, it includes the major themes and people. On a technical note, I have written a limerick for each of the 150 Psalms, and in the case of the 119th Psalm, one limerick per section. If there are glaring omissions, then I apologise in advance – for I am no great theologian but merely a retired Anglican Vicar. Even so, I would be glad to receive comments, criticisms, and corrections. I invite readers to submit their own limericks as well, which might be considered for future editions of *"The Bible in Limerick Verse."*

This afternoon, I sat down and read the whole work in a couple of hours – which is the amount of time that people often have to wait in departure lounges at airports for plane connections. If it were as easy to read as some people say it is, then I would love to see copies of it in hotel rooms, airport lounges, doctors' and dentists' waiting rooms, libraries, churches, and schools, as well as in people's homes.

"Have this mind in you, which was also in Christ Jesus" said St. Paul *(Philippians 2:5)* And, as the Scriptures helped to form the mind of Jesus, then my aim is that *"The Bible in Limerick Verse"*

may *also* help to form the minds of people in the 21st Century who may have little or no understanding of what the Bible is all about.

Finally, I would like to record my thanks to Peter Wright, priest, lecturer at my Theological College, for inspiring me to get excited about the Bible; to so many people who have made constructive comments and suggestions for improvement; to my publisher, John Hunt, for his enthusiasm and wisdom; and last, but not least, to my wife Doreen for her tireless support and encouragement.

Christopher W.H. Goodwins
Isleham
26 April 2006

Foreword
by The Dean of St. Paul's, the Venerable Dr John Moses

How do we enable people to read the Bible and discover its meaning for themselves? This is the all-important question that lies behind Christopher Goodwins' work in recent years in using Limerick verse to bring home to a new generation the stories, the mysteries, the insights and the teaching of the Bible.

I am glad to commend *The Bible in Limerick Verse* to all who find this book and attempt to use it. I want to say to every reader: Don't be in a hurry. Do not be deceived by the apparently simple approach that has been adopted. Give yourself time to read – perhaps to read aloud – to reflect, and to find for yourself the abiding truths that lie at the heart of our Christian faith.

Introduction

What is a limerick?

A limerick is a five-line verse, the lines of which rhyme as follows:
A A B B A, such as:

The Bible in Rhyme is a book	A
At which you should take a good look.	A
This Anglican vicar	B
Has made it much quicker	B
To use as a bait on your hook!	A

Most limericks are designed to be funny, and some are extremely bawdy. But this doesn't prevent the use of the 5-line AABBA verse to express serious subjects, such as the Bible.

To the contrary, there is a wealth of poetry in verses of varying numbers of lines, on all sorts of subjects: but this doesn't preclude biblical themes being written in verse of the same metre, which is exactly what hymns are.

Most hymns are written in four-line verses, and no one sees anything wrong in that; and I know of at least one hymn in 5-line verses, not with limerick verse metre, but definitely with the limerick-rhyming system of AABBA – *(in Ancient & Modern Revised Hymnal Number 382) as follows:*

Praise to the Lord, the Almighty, the King of creation;	A
O my soul, praise Him, for He is thy health and salvation:	A
All ye who hear,	B
Now to His temple draw near,	B
Joining in glad adoration.	A

Why should the devil have *all the best tunes*,
and why should the devil have *all the best poetry* -
and that applies also to *limericks!*

What's the difference between a Bible in *verse*, and a Bible in *limerick*?

A limerick is no different from any other form of poetry except in the number of lines and the rhyming sequence of those lines.

However, because of the rhyming sequence (A A B B A) it seems to make limerick verses a little easier to memorise.

And because the limericks in *"The Bible In Limerick Verse"* substantially *summarise* the pages of the Bible, it considerably reduces the number of words to be read. This should be of great help to someone who might go on to have a look at the Bible (proper) for the first time.

As an example, have a look at Psalm 23: In the Revised Version *(which has been my working bible for the past 42 years)* Psalm 23 totals 119 words, 125 words in the 1662 BCP version, and 116 in the NIV version – **i.e., an average of 120 words.**

However, *in limerick verse,* the 23rd Psalm is summarised into **a mere 34 words** *i.e., a quarter of the size* – as follows:

Psalm 23
The Lord is my shepherd. He leads me.   401
Beside the still waters He feeds me.
I walk without fear.
Rod and staff show He's near!
The feast, at His table, soon will be!

I consider that the above limerick (number 401) still expresses the original text with a degree of faithfulness, while at the same time making the verse extremely memorable. My hope is that anybody reading the limerick version may become curious enough to compare what the 23rd Psalm actually looks like in *the real Bible,* and therefore, as a result, will absorb a huge amount of the Bible in so doing.

No one has succeeded in putting the whole Bible into 1001 limericks before, and certainly **no one has ever attempted to include The Old Testament and the Apocrypha, with the New Testament, in Limerick Verse IN ONE BOOK.** *That's* the difference!

How to understand Biblical references

1. **Each Limerick has a** *BIBLICAL REFERENCE, for example:*
Genesis 3: 1-6 *[This means the book in the Bible called Genesis, chapter 3, verses 1 to 6]*

Along came the serpent. 'Don't wait!
You may eat the fruit, so I state!'
It did look so nice,
And it just took a trice!
The damage was done! They both ate!

2. **And each limerick is** *NUMBERED,* **to make it easy to look up,** *for example:*

Matthew 2: 9-10
They followed the star all the way
To Bethlehem, where the child lay
In the darkness that night.
When they saw him, the sight
Was one of exceeding great joy!

756
[This is the limerick number]

3. **In the** *INDEX OF PEOPLE* **you'll find**

Adam   6, 12-13, 20
This means that *Adam* is mentioned in *limericks numbered 6, 12 & 13, and 20.*
For example, number 6:

Genesis 2: 18 – 24
The intricate parts took their places
Right up to the first human races.
Whoever they were
Eve and **Adam** infer
God made us all from the same faces.

6

If you're new to the Bible, I hope this helps!

Limerick lists

Numbers refer to number of limerick.

Books of the Bible

New Testament

Matthew	753
Mark	794
Luke	817
John	848
Acts	894
Romans	910
1 Corinthians	926
2 Corinthians	935
Galatians	939
Ephesians	942
Philippians	945
Colossians	948
1 Thessalonians	952
2 Thessalonians	955
1 Timothy	956
2 Timothy	959
Titus	962
Philemon	964
Hebrews	965
James	974
1 Peter	976
2 Peter	982
1 John	983
2 John	988
3 John	989
Jude	990
Revelation	991

Bible books, in alphabetical order

Acts	894	Habakkuk	683
Amos	662	Haggai	687
Baruch	719	Hebrews	965
Bel and the Dragon	730	Hosea	653
1 Chronicles	345	Isaiah	567
2 Chronicles	348	James	974
1 Corinthians	926	Jeremiah	600
2 Corinthians	935	Job	370
Colossians	948	Joel	656
Daniel	629	John	848
Deuteronomy	194	1 John	983
Ecclesiastes	556	2 John	988
Ecclesiasticus	715	3 John	989
Ephesians	942	Jonah	669
1 Esdras	698	Joshua	210
2 Esdras	703	Jude	990
Esther	365	Judges	221
Exodus	96	Judith	708
Ezekiel	615	1 Kings	292
Ezra	350	2 Kings	326
Galatians	939	Lamentations	612
Genesis	1	Leviticus	164

Luke	817	Ruth	244
1 Maccabees	739	1 Samuel	248
2 Maccabees	748	2 Samuel	276
Malachi	694	The History of Susannah	725
Mark	794	The Prayer of Manasses	737
Matthew	753	The Rest of Esther	711
Micah	678	The Song of Songs	564
Nahum	681	The Song of the	
Nehemiah	355	Three Holy Children	722
Numbers	168	1 Thessalonians	952
Obadiah	668	2 Thessalonians	955
1 Peter	976	1 Timothy	956
2 Peter	982	2 Timothy	959
Philemon	964	The Wisdom of Solomon	712
Philippians	945	Titus	962
Proverbs	550	Tobit	704
Psalms	379	Zechariah	689
Revelation	991	Zephaniah	685
Romans	910		

People of the Bible

Aaron   118, 156-157, 174, 181, 455, 532
Abel   14-17
Abijah   315
Abijam   317
Abimalech   51, 229
Abiram   182
Abishag [Abi-S]   292, 296
Abner   277
Abram, [Abraham, Abie, Abe]   33-43, 45, 47-48, 51-61, 68, 106-107, 718, 753, 858
Absalom   287-288
Adam   6, 12-13, 20
Adonijah   296
Advocate   984
Ahab   323, 325, 335
Ahasuerus   365, 368

Ahaziah [A'ziah]   325-326
Ahimelech   271
Ahinoam   273
Alpha & Omega   991
Ammon   50, 286-287
Amos   662-663, 665-667, 678
Ananias   904
Andrew   797
Antichrist   998
Antiochus Epiphanes   740
Apostles   895, 897
Artaxerxes   355
Asa   317
Assyria, king of   338
Augustine   910
Azariah [Az, Abednego]   630, 631,638
Baal   228, 320-321, 335
Baker (Pharaoh's)   87

Uzziah, king   574
Vashti, queen   366
Wesley, John   910
Witch of Endor   274-275
Witnesses   970

YAHWEH   116
Zephaniah son of Cushi   685
Zerah   84
Zipporah [Zippy]   102-103
Zophar   375

Themes of the Bible

Abandoned   400
Abraham's death   60
Abroad   18, 114, 379, 906
Adam & Eve   6-13,
Adore   339, 360, 505, 818, 938, 966
Adversity   516
Air   523, 897, 952
Alarm   174, 773
Alms   705, 773
Amen   268, 345, 417, 690, 718
Anger   260, 263, 658
Animals   148, 428, 482, 546, 568, 967
Anoint   155, 257, 261, 294, 312, 314, 325, 532, 859, 975
Answer(s)   257-258, 306, 369, 382, 684, 701
Ants   554
Apocalypse   652, 703
Apocrypha   752
Apples   551
Arm(s)   239, 566, 588
Armour   265, 325, 543, 943
Arrow   325, 435, 526
Ashes   373
Ass (donkey)   187, 236, 691, 819, 863
Authority   780
Awe   454
Baby, babies   41, 99, 247-248, 284, 298-299, 680, 819

Baptism   762, 848, 902, 904, 914
Barbecue   892
Bare feet   106, 214
Battle(s)   41, 123, 142, 190, 193, 195, 214, 218, 260, 288, 543
Bear(s)   329, 646
Beard   282
Beauty   83, 283, 367, 474, 565
Bed   129, 251, 286, 330, 556, 798, 801
Bees   234, 971
Benedicite   724
Benjamin's cup   91
Bereaved   770
Bird(s)   2, 26, 462, 482, 523, 561, 776, 835
Bishop   958, 963
Bless(ings)   34, 41, 54, 66-67, 95, 149, 167, 172, 197, 244, 296, 301, 363, 378, 380-381, 407, 419, 445, 450, 490, 496-497, 527, 531-533, 769-770, 816, 976, 979
Blind   466, 584, 591, 706, 859
Blood   17, 80, 119, 129, 153, 334, 660, 927, 943
Boils   124, 373
Bones   625
Book(s)   164, 339, 436, 366, 530, 562, 567, 703, 712-713, 719-720, 730, 737, 739, 780, 826, 893, 961

Selected Christian themes

Peter's affirmation   810
Resurrection, Easter   887, 890
Saul's (Paul) Baptism   904
Thomas   889
Thomas' affirmation   889

Trials   875-877
Trinity   852
Upper Room   885, 888-889
Venite, the   445
Whitsun/Pentecost   894-895

Places in the Bible

Adullam's cave   272
Alexandria   712
Ammon   50
Asia Minor   990
Asian Churches   992
Assyria   338, 682
Babylon   344, 359, 536, 629, 635,
   681, 704, 738
Bethel   67, 311, 329, 336, 665
Bethlehem   244, 261, 755-756,
   819
Canaan   33, 40, 57, 131, 180, 191,
   195, 210, 220, 483
Capernaum   766, 794
Cave   57, 272, 322, 668
Chaldaea   683, 721
City of David   278
Court(s)   92, 462, 729, 876
Damascus   331, 903
Dan   311, 336
Decapolis   809
Desert   137, 583-584
Earth   2, 21, 67, 249, 347, 386,
   396-397, 425, 443, 445, 447,
   514, 553, 566, 609, 771, 775,
   859, 900, 921, 999, 1000
Egypt   36-37, 53, 82, 89, 94, 96,
   99, 101, 109, 118, 131, 134, 136,
   159, 176, 181, 483, 492, 759
Endor   274
Ephesus   958, 992
Ethiopia   365, 902
Galeed   74

Galilee   761, 766
Gath   289
Gilgal   259
Greece   651-652, 719
Heaven   2, 57, 67, 328, 392, 397,
   435, 447, 477, 491, 508, 538,
   592, 609, 647, 649, 751, 775,
   778, 786, 870, 899, 947, 994,
   997, 1000
Hebron   219
Hill(s)   280, 393, 402, 476, 492,
   520, 597, 769
India   365
Israel   96-98, 103, 107, 115, 124,
   133, 136, 142, 149, 155-156,
   158, 163-164, 168, 170, 172,
   174, 180, 191, 193, 196, 198,
   202, 218, 220-221, 228, 253,
   255, 264, 278, 289-290, 305,
   335, 338, 340, 342, 344-345,
   346, 348, 350, 362, 431, 450-
   454, 456, 459, 461, 465, 477,
   483-485, 492, 523-525, 530,
   534-535, 548, 564, 598, 601,
   605, 607-608, 610, 613, 615,
   617, 619, 627, 652-653, 656,
   666-667, 676, 683, 718, 738,
   744, 749, 752, 817-818
Israel [Jacob]   75-76, 94-95
Jericho   211-212, 214-216, 832
Jerusalem   278, 280, 295, 302,
   309-310, 317-318, 324, 349,
   351, 355, 359, 457, 465, 521,

Abbreviations used

Limerick version in left hand column, Bible name in right hand column.

Abe	Abraham	Shad	Hananiah
Abednego	Azariah	Shadrach	Hananiah
Abie	Abraham	Sol	Solomon
Abi-S	Abishag	Susie	Susannah
Abram	Abraham	Zippy	Zipporah
Az	Azariah		
A'ziah	Ahaziah		
Becky	Rebekah		
Belteshazzar	Daniel		
Dan	Daniel		
El	Elijah the Tishbite		
Ez	Ezekiel		
Ezek	Ezekiel		
Gol	Goliath		
Han	Hananiah		
Ike	Isaac		
Jake	Jacob		
Jerry	Jeroboam		
Jerry	Jeremiah		
Jo	Joseph		
Jon	Jonathan		
MacBee	Maccabaeus		
Maccs	Maccabaeus		
Matt	Mattathias		
Matty	Mattathias		
Mesh	Mishael		
Meshach	Mishael		
Mo	Moses		
Neb	Nebuchadnezzar		
Nebbie	Nebuchadnezzar		
Neh	Nehemiah		
Sam	Samson		
Sam	Samuel		

To write your own limericks

If you have a far better rhyme,
That sums up the Bible text, I'm
Quite willing to say
That your verse wins the day
And I'll try to include it, next time!

The Limerick Bible hymn

1. We praise God every hour of the day.
   God's Spirit has so much to say
   To us, and our friends.
   Every message God sends
   Is pointing us in the right way!

2. Don't let *The Good Book* gather dust.
   Keep reading, and don't let it rust!
   Soon things become clear
   As we all persevere –
   And in Jesus place all of our trust.

3. So, just let Jesus play His full part
   By really preparing your heart.
   You'll find that in prayer
   Jesus is always there,
   And He'll help you to make a fresh start!

4. Praise God's Holy Spirit, the same –
   Our Father – in whom Jesus came:
   We need You so much,
   And we crave for Your touch,
   And we want to be Yours! That's our aim!

THE LIMERICK BIBLE HYMN

there, And He'll help you to make a fresh start! 4. Praise God's Ho- ly

Spir- it, the same - Our Fa- ther - in whom Je- sus came:

We need You so much, And we crave for Your touch, And we want to be

Yours! That's our aim!

The Limericks

The Old Testament

If you want to know how we began   1
The clues are in Genesis, man!
There was nothing at first
Till the universe burst
On infinity, as God's plan.

From nothing, God made the whole lot,   2
Put heaven and earth on the spot.
He made grass and fruit,
Sun and moon – it's a hoot!
With birds, fish, and insects. That's what!

Then cattle, and all creeping things,   3
And creatures that fly with their wings.
His image He gave
For mankind, but *'I save*
Day seven, for rest that it brings.'

He saw what He'd made, as He would,   4
And knew what He'd made was so good.
'It's now up to you,'
He said. *'It's all for you –*
So care for it, please, as you should!'

To understand life, it seems right   5
That God made the lot – day and night!
The universe grew
As His Spirit moved too!
Read on, and you'll meet *The True Light!*

The intricate parts took their places 6
Right up to the first human races.
Whoever they were
Eve and Adam infer
God made us all from the same faces.

With everything beautiful there 7
Temptation was too great to bear.
The fruit of the tree
Gave them knowledge, you see:
Choose evil or good – yes, it's fair!

Along came the serpent. 'Don't wait! 8
You may eat the fruit, so I state!'
It did look so nice,
And it just took a trice!
The damage was done! They both ate!

But then, in the cool of the day 9
They both heard the voice of God say –
'Where are you, you two?'
'We were naked, and threw
Some fig leaves on, and hid away!'

'But how did you know you were bare?' 10
Asked God. *'Have you eaten fruit where*
I told you not to?'
'Oh – the serpent said You
Won't mind! We accepted the dare!'

'Well, now you must pay for your sin! 11
These clothes are for you to get in!
And so you must toil
As you till all the soil,
And dust-unto-dust will begin!'

So that spelt the end of the fun –   12
Our work in life had just begun!
Hence Adam and Eve
Had, from Eden, to leave!
And this is how *'The Fall' was* done!

Yes – Adam and Eve had the two   13
Sons. Cain was the first, the one who
Was a tiller of soil
Who, with sweat and with toil
Did rather successfully, too!

Their second son, Abel, was deep   14
Into farming, and rearing sheep.
Their friendship fell out
When Cain began to shout
At Abel, and that made him weep.

Cain offered his first-fruits, and said   15
'Accept this, Lord!' But God instead
Accepted the other
That came from his brother –
And made Cain wish Abel were dead!

Cain took it into his own head   16
That Abel would be better dead.
He slew him one day,
When God questioned him. *'Hey –
I'm not Abel's keeper!'* he said!

The Lord said, *'Where's Abel? Tell me!'* 17
But Cain's guilty secret, you see
Was there to be found
In the blood on the ground.
Thus Cain became fugitive, he!

So Cain was marked-out by the Lord –   18
Who vowed that when Cain went abroad
Whoever first found him
Should kill him, or wound him.
Hence eastward Cain fled, towards Nod.

Lamech had kids, three or four   19
Like Jabal, the cattle-man, or
Jubal, musician,
And Tubal-Cain – fission
Was his skill, with metals galore.

For relatives from Adam's stable,   20
A genealogical table
Describes at great length
Who begat whom. Its strength
Should help you find out, if you're able.

On earth families spread like wild fire,   21
And some ignored God. *'Why enquire*
What happens if we
Get too clever?' 'You'll see!'
Said God, as the rain became dire.

One family planted its trust   22
So firmly in God. *'If we must,'*
Said Noah, *'We'll go build*
A boat – and not get killed
By floodwaters!' – He had it sussed!

The others stood by and just jeered   23
At Noah, who waved back – and cheered
When flood drowned the baddies –
But not lass or laddies,
Nor wife, nor his family! Weird!

He'd taken on board all he could　　24
Of all living creatures who would
Get into the ark
Not afraid of the dark!
Including a raven. That's good!

GENESIS 8

As God made His point, the rain stopped,　　25
And onto Mount Ararat dropped
The ark. All within it
Cried, *'Praise God! We've done it!'*
And onto dry land out they popped!

GENESIS 8: 8

A year had passed by, when a dove　　26
Flew out on a mission. *'My love,'*
Noah told his missus,
'This bird' – between kisses –
'Will come back with hope from above!'

GENESIS 8: 11

The olive branch, quite fresh and green　　27
For twelve months had never been seen.
'This means we are saved!'
Noah said, and he raved
With joy, and said *'Trust God, I mean!'*

GENESIS 9: 1-17

The rainbow had signalled God's end　　28
To flooding. So now they could send
The whole boatload out.
'No more rain!' God said, *'Nowt! –*
It's a promise I'll always defend!'

GENESIS 9: 18-28

Lived rather a long time, did Noah.　　29
He had only three sons, not four.
Shem, and brother Ham
And then Japeth. Yes, Ma'am!
These ones were his family. Oh, coo er!

'Go, multiply!' – God said, 'and bud,   30
But Noah – watch out for the mud!'
They numbered so many
Became two a penny –
The ones who'd survived from the flood.

GENESIS 11: 1–5

At that time, they all spoke the same.   31
They got on quite well, but became
So greedy for power
They each built a tower.
The higher, the greater their fame!

GENESIS 11: 6–9

God saw through their pride and their plots.   32
One language He turned into lots.
They suddenly saw
That their power was no more –
Their babbling was just like a tot's!

GENESIS 11: 29

Abram went out and he married   33
Sarai. Both of them tarried
In Ur, till God said
'It is time that you led
The family to Canaan!' He hurried.

GENESIS 12: 1–3

Said God, 'You'll do just what I say!'   34
Abram said, 'Lord, no other way!'
'OK, then! That's fine,
All your blessings are mine!'
The nation emerged, day by day.

GENESIS 12: 6–7

At Shechem, Abe heard the Lord say   35
'I'll give you this land here, one day!'
So he built an altar.
His faith did not falter
As Abram then went on his way.

God promised that one day, he would   36
Give Abram his own land for good.
But now, south he went
Into Egypt as sent
Where famine was raging. No food!

The Pharaoh of Egypt showed lust   37
For Abram's wife. He was nonplussed
When God sent a plague!
He could not now renege –
As Abram then set off in trust.

With Sarai and brother Lot   38
Abe went south, and so soon forgot
The past. Then at Mamre
An altar built. *'Hey we*
By far prefer this building plot!'

Abe said, with a commanding voice   39
To Lot, *'You go left. That's your choice!*
And I'll take the right!
So I bid you goodnight!'
They parted, amidst lots of noise.

So Lot chose the Jordan Plain east,   40
Abram chose Canaan. The least
He could do was to say
'I'm so glad I'm this way!
Build an altar! Let's have a feast!'

Poor Lot had a really rough time,   41
And got caught in battle and slime.
To rescue him Abie
Saved Lot, brother, baby.
Melchizadek blessed him in rhyme.

At that stage, poor Abe had no heir. 42
He, Sarai, both near despair!
But God had a plan
For this patriarch man.
'Believe me, Abe!' God said. So there!

'Your family will be as the stars – 43
So great in a very few years!'
'How can I believe it?'
Asked Abie, 'I've planned it!'
Said God, 'You can drop all your fears!'

'Your future depends on a girl – 44
A maid, who's called Hagar, will hurl
Herself in your life
She'll be your second wife.'
Bore Ishmael, fair-haired, with curl.

This Covenant came into force 45
And Abram replied, almost hoarse,
'I'll never forsake You
Dear God, I will take You!'
'OK, Abraham! Yes, of course!'

'There's one thing I want you to do,' 46
Said God, 'And it's all up to you!
Just circumcise men
Eight days old, please, and then
It marks you as mine! Yes – it's true!'

'Your Sarai's 'Sarah' from now 47
And she'll be a mummy too!' 'How?'
Asked Abie. 'We're old!'
'Oh – you just won't be told!'
Scolded God. 'Have more faith!' – Oh wow!

As Sarah now overheard this,   48
She laughed till she cried! *I'm a Miss –*
And far too decrepid
For motherhood!' Tepid
Remark, but gave Abie a kiss.

'There's one thing you must not do – not!   49
In Sodom the men want you, Lot!
But quit there for Zoar,
Don't look back, but go! – Er –
Bad news! Your wife's now become salt!

That night, Lot drank far too much wine.   50
His daughter lay with him till nine.
The other one too –
Well aware what they'd do!
'Now Moab and Ammon are thine!'

Now Abraham, curious mister,   51
Said *(wife)* Sarah was just his *sister.*
King Abimalech
Dreamt he took a big peck,
But woke up so glad he'd not kissed her!

Old Sarah conceived, had a child –   52
Delighted her Abraham wild!
He took a sharp knife
As he said to his wife
'God marks Isaac now, undefiled.'

But trouble blew up in Abe's camp   53
When Hagar, his Gyppie-slave vamp
Began mocking Sarah,
And tore out her hair-a:
'You've got to get rid of that tramp!'

God now put old Abe to the test.   54
'Your son, Isaac, has to go west!
So, like a young goat
Put a knife to his throat
And slay him, so you may be blessed!'

Thus Abraham did as God said   55
His knife poised to kill Isaac dead –
When God changed his mind:
'You've such faith! Look behind!
There's a ram in the hedge. Him instead!'

So God had led Abe to the brink,   56
But at the last moment, said *'Think*
Of the Pact we have made!
So Abe, don't be afraid!
Forever! A Covenant-link!'

Sarah, a hundred-two-seven   57
Departed this life. Went to heaven.
In Machpelah cave
Abie made Sarah's grave
At Mamre *(that's Hebron)*, Canaan.

Abe sent off his servant, to look   58
For a wife, son Isaac could hook.
At Nahor he found one
Rebekah, a sound one,
A girl who would make a great cook!

As dowry changed hands, so she went   59
With Abe's servant, camels and tent.
Isaac knelt there and prayed
Till he saw the parade,
And *'Becky,'* for whom he had sent.

Abraham married again.   60
Family increased by the ten.
Then to Isaac, gave all
But Abe died in the Fall –
Was buried at Machpelah plain.

Abe's two-handled family thrived.   61
And dozens of children survived!
Rebekah bore twins
But remarked, amidst grins
'Rough and smooth, Isaac!' Uncontrived!

Ike's favourite twin, hairy Esau   62
Would hunt. But Jacob his twin bro'
Was Rebekah's pet,
Preferred home life. And yet
Problems accrued. You know *who* for!

Now Jacob had hunted all day,   63
And dinner was ready. Hey, hey!
Quite faint, Esau traded
His birthright, and faded
Away, leaving Jacob to play!

As Isaac's prosperity grew   64
So God became close to him. True!
He made friends with all
But his eyesight did pall:
He no longer knew who was who!

Rebekah had hatched-up a plot   65
To fool Isaac over a pot
Of stew she had cooked.
Camouflaged so it looked
Like Jacob was Esau. He's not!

While Jacob received his dad's blessing 66
Bro Esau was livid. No messing!
The plot came to light,
And he vowed he just might
Kill brother! Blow Jacob's caressing!

So Jacob succeeded by guile 67
Obtaining dad's blessing, but while
He dreamed at Bethel
Of a ladder, which fell
From heaven to earth – mile on mile!

The angels were up and then down 68
The ladder from 'Top Of The Town.'
'I'm Abraham's God,'
God said, *'and Isaac's! – Nod*
If I'm Yours, dear Jacob! Don't frown!'

This Laban's two daughters were Leah 69
And Rachel. Then Jacob came near.
'I'll work seven years
For your Rachel! I'm hers!'
Laban had another idea!

On Jacob, Laban played a trick! 70
Jake married the wrong daughter. *'Quick –*
I'll serve seven years
More, if I can be hers –
Your Rachel!' The whole joke was sick!

Eventually, Rachel conceived, 71
And Joseph was born. She believed
That God heard her prayer
And allowed her to bear
A son. She was no longer peeved!

For two decades Laban served Jacob, 72
But then got quite fed up with the job.
Jake left him one day,
Took his family away,
As young Rachel went out on the rob.

She stole Jacob's gods called *teraphim*, 73
And hid them, so Jake wouldn't find 'em.
Some boundary stones
Jake set up. Then he moans,
'If they cross this line, then I'll harm 'em!'

'Galeed' was the name Laban gave it, 74
And *'Mizpah'* the way he explained it.
'The Lord will watch you,
And between us – it's true –
Our paths will not cross again. Get it?'

All night Jacob wrestled in vain 75
But God pricked his conscience again.
'From now on, your name
Will be Israel. A shame
Your hip has been put to such strain!'

'I'll say this to you just once more,' 76
God said to young Jacob – *'Encore*
It's Israel – your name –
You'll achieve such great fame!
Your kingdom will grow by the score!'

This Joseph was Jacob's young son. 77
Designed him a coloured coat, one
Which made him stand out,
Caused his brothers to pout
With envy. 'Twas no longer fun!

It didn't help when Joseph dreamed　　　78
That wheat and cows, sun and moon, deemed
To fall down before him:
'Your brothers – ignore them!'
Was what Joseph's message had seemed.

Directly to Shechem they raced,　　　79
The flock needed feeding, in haste.
Their devious plan
Was to sell Joseph, man!
Then say he was dead! Such bad taste!

His coat they threw into a pit　　　80
With blood on, so folk would think it
Was where Joseph died.
Its bright colours outside
Would signal Jo's death, quite a bit!

They brought the coat back to his dad.　　　81
'Look what has become of the lad!'
They said, between tears,
Making Jacob's worst fears
Believe Jo was dead! Jake went mad!

But Joseph was safe in the hand　　　82
Of Midianites' travelling band.
To Egypt they came
And sold Joseph – the same –
To Potiphar, Pharaoh's right-hand.

Said Judah to Onan, *'Your duty*　　　83
Is clearly to father a beauty!'
His nerve failed him when
He *spilled-out,* there and then –
And died in the act! Naughty naughty!

GENESIS 38: 12–30

Her father-in-law, namely Judah   84
Produced twins for Tamar. What cruder!
Red thread on his wrist
Zerah should be born first,
But Perez emerged as the leader!

GENESIS 39: 1–20

More intrigue. Wife of Potiphar   85
Seduced Jo – a steamy affair!
Producing his clothes
She said, *'Evidence shows*
He's the culprit! Jail him! Ha ha!'

GENESIS 39:21–23

In prison did Joseph so well,   86
Promoted him fast, so they tell.
Intrigues nearly sunk him.
No one could debunk him
With God on his side, they just fell!

GENESIS 40

The butler and baker fell foul   87
Of Pharaoh. But then, wise old owl –
At Joseph's entreating
The butler kept meeting.
The baker he hanged! Let's all howl!

GENESIS 41

Pharaoh kept dreaming. *'What's this?'*   88
So Joseph interpreted. *'Giss*
A mo to make plans,
And store wheat in our barns –
And we'll give the famine a miss!'

GENESIS 42

His plans were so obviously neat   89
That people begged Egypt, to eat!
'Don't starve our poor nation
But give us salvation!'
His family, soon, Jo would meet.

GENESIS 43

Now Joseph soon saw who they were.　　　90
They still didn't know him. *'Please Sir,'*
They said, as he spoke,
'You're a very nice bloke!'
A test was on hand to make sure.

GENESIS 44

In Benjamin's sack, was a cup　　　91
That Joseph had hidden – straight up!
They found it too late
As they journeyed till eight –
He'd have to be hostage – the pup!

GENESIS 45: 4

But Joseph's pretence could not last.　　　92
'I'm Joseph!' he owned up. *'I've passed*
Many years here at court
And you – all of you – thought
I'd died in that pit you me cast.'

GENESIS 45: 16–28

Pharaoh and Joseph were glad,　　　93
And so was his family. *'The lad*
Has done himself proud,
So we're all now allowed
To tell the good news to our dad!'

GENESIS 46: 1–7

So Israel determined, *'I'll see*　　　94
What my sons reported to me!'
To Egypt he moved
With the family he loved –
No happier dad could there be!

GENESIS 49

Disputes followed blessings galore,　　　95
But finally, Israel was sure.
He took his last breath
As he went to his death –
His family at peace, all the more.

> When Joseph had died, things got worse –   96
> The Pharaoh decided to curse
> All the Israelite folk
> There in Egypt – no joke!
> And got them brick-making! So terse!

> The midwives were named – Shiphrah, Puah,   97
> It seems there were only the two – er –
> In all Israel!
> They worked flat out! Well –
> What *else* could two midwives do? Coo, er!

> He ordered those midwives to kill   98
> All Israelite boys born, but still
> To let the girls be.
> But the orders, you see
> Were all disobeyed, if you will!

> A Levite girl, after awhile,   99
> Had baby son. Then by the Nile
> She set him afloat
> In a bullrush-made boat
> For his future in Egypt in style!

> The Pharaoh's young daughter passed by.   100
> *'Whatever is this, I espy?'*
> She picked up the boy,
> Cuddled him like a toy
> And named him *her Moses*. My, my!

> When Moses grew up, he inspected   101
> Some injustice, never expected.
> An Egyptian bully
> He slew, wholly, fully!
> To Midian fled undetected.

He lay low until one fine day   102
A beautiful girl came his way.
'Oh Zipporah, dear
Be my wife! Yes, right here!'
They married without more delay!

Before long, a young son she bore   103
Called Gershom, *'The Israelite for*
A stranger,' he said
'In a strange land, I'm led!'
And Zippy and Moses said, *'Cor!'*

Now Moses was tending the sheep   104
One day when his conscience went *'Bleep!'*
'I'm God!' said the voice,
'And you now have the choice –
The God of your fathers to keep!'

While tending his sheep, Moses saw   105
A huge bush on fire. *'What's the score?'*
He thought, as a voice
Called to him, *'Moses!' (twice)*
'Right here!' – Moses said – *'Yes! What for?'*

The Lord said, *'Stay there! Don't get near!*   106
Barefoot where you stand, you'll revere!'
On holy ground trod
Moses. *'I am the God*
Of Abe, Ike, and Jake – is that clear?'

'I am the God of your crowd –   107
Of Abraham, Isaac – I vowed –
And Jacob as well,
And I want you to tell
Every Israelite here. Now! Aloud!'

'I've heard your prayer here from on high,   108
I want you to know I'm nearby!'
'So what is Your name?'
Moses asked, heart aflame:
'I AM WHO I AM! It's no lie!'

'My plan is to set you all free   109
From Egypt, and soon you will see
If you follow my word
To the letter you heard
From I AM WHO I AM – that's me!'

'So how will they know that it's true?'   110
Asked Moses, of God. 'Well – when you
Strike hard with your rod –
As a snake from the sod
It will be!' 'Beat that!' – Moses said – 'Phew!'

If that wasn't funny enough,   111
The next trick would call Moses' bluff.
His hand like a leper –
Looked something like pepper!
But then, back to normal! Just rough!

'It's My way to tell you the truth'   112
Said God, 'You're no longer a youth!
So do as I say
And I'll show you the way,
And no one will say you're uncouth!'

So Moses kept on at Pharaoh   113
And nagged him, 'Release people, so!
'We'll only be gone
For a feast.' ('Twas a con!)
'And over the Red Sea we'll go!'

But Pharaoh increased their hard task.   114
'It's no good you coming to ask
To travel abroad
Just to worship Your Lord! –
So wipe off the grin from your mask!'

'Just get making bricks without straw!'   115
Said Pharaoh! *'And make plenty more!'*
The Israelites worked
Hard, and nobody shirked,
But they yearned to show Moses the door!

God said, *'Moses, this is My name*   116
So holy, but don't take the blame!
It sounds like wind blowing.
'YAHWEH' gets you going!
The patriarchs called Me the same!'

To Moses, God said, *'This is it!*   117
And now you will see bit by bit
What power I possess!
So obey Me, unless
In slavery you want to sit!'

So Moses and Aaron did tricks   118
To impress the Pharaoh, and fix
Their exodus out
Of Egypt, no doubt!
Then God planned a nastier mix!

The first plague turned river to blood.   119
No water to drink. *'If we could*
Please leave for three days?'
'Just stay put!' Pharaoh says,
But Moses continued to brood.

'Just see how you like plagues of frogs!'   120
Said Moses to Pharaoh. 'It jogs
My memory here
That you might disappear!
So just you stay put! Dirty dogs!'

The next plague turned out to be lice.   121
Pharaoh said, *'Moses - that's not nice!'*
His magic-men said
'Our spells kill lice dead!'
They didn't. So then came the flies!

The flies plagued old Pharaoh right cruel.   122
'What is Moses up to, the fool?'
'Just let us go free
We'll come back, just you see!'
Said Moses, to Pharaoh, so cool.

Despite Moses' efforts to rattle   123
Old Pharaoh, it still left the cattle.
'Watch me!' Moses said
As he nodded his head –
'This plague will be worse than a battle!'

Each time Pharaoh changed his mind, he   124
Refused Moses' Israelites' plea.
So just for his toils
Pharaoh came out in boils
And *that* stung his pride, don't you see!

He still wouldn't let Moses go,   125
So hail, fire, and thunder, and snow
Was what God sent next –
As you read in the text.
But Pharaoh said, *'No! – No! No! No!'*

'How about locusts, instead?'   126
Said Moses to Pharaoh. 'You said
That we could go free,
But these plagues came, you see –
Because you would rather us dead!'

'I tell you what,' said Moses then,   127
'We'll blot out daylight, won't we, men!'
With Pharaoh enveloped,
Thick darkness developed!
'When will this all end, Moses, when?'

The time came for Moses to act.   128
Old Pharaoh had broken his pact.
'At midnight, yes we
Will be crossing the Sea!'
Said Moses. Laughed Pharaoh, then cracked!

'Instruct everybody,' Mo said   129
'And get everyone out of bed.
'Have roast lamb before,
Paint red blood on the door,
So God's Angel will pass overhead!'

The doorposts without any mark   130
Were earmarked for slaughter in dark.
But those who survived
By the Sea had arrived,
Awaiting instructions in park.

To navigate well, Moses saw   131
A pillar of fire by night, or
A cloud in the day
To help them make their way
From Egypt to Canaan, and more!

The people were all at a loss.   132
'However shall we get across?'
But then – hand on heart –
Moses waved Sea apart,
And praised, *'God Almighty! You're Boss!'*

The people crossed over in glee   133
On dry land, in midst of the Sea.
But Pharaoh raged on
With the Israelites gone –
'Get them back!' yelled Pharaoh, *'To me!'*

His chariots came hard on their heel,   134
But mud just stuck fast to the wheel.
'I think we are doomed!'
Said Egyptians, entombed.
They drowned in the Sea. No big deal!

Then Moses sang praise to the Lord: 135
'I thank You for keeping Your word!'
The women with timbrels
Sang, danced, to their cymbals
'We're free from old Pharaoh! Thank God!'

The prophetess, Miriam, she   136
Danced, and shook her timbrel in glee!
'The Lord, He's been good
And has quite understood
That Israel from Egypt should flee!'

The trouble about such a journey   137
Showed Moses the need for attorney.
'The desert's so dry
If we don't drink, we die!'
As people complained, *'We'll go loony!'*

The waters of Marah were banned,   138
But God had the matter in hand:
As Moses threw tree
Into water. *'Yippee!'* –
'Just drink all you like, hand in hand!'

Then came the grave matter of hunger.   139
'We really can't go any longer!'
'Let no one complain!'
Just then, quails came like rain
As Moses *dispatched* a scaremonger.

Next morning, when Moses arose   140
The ground there was covered like snows.
'Here's manna to eat!'
Moses said, *'It's a treat!*
Like wafers and honey it goes!'

Then came a serious complaint: 141
'If we don't get water – we'll faint!'
So, using his rod
Moses struck rock. *'Oh God*
Please help us!' *'You thirsty? – I ain't!'*

More battles took place all too soon.   142
And Moses was weary at noon.
'We'll prop up his hand,
So they all understand
That Israel will win, and not swoon!'

Poor Moses had too much to do,   143
His father-in-law sensed it, too.
'You delegate power'
He said, *'right from this hour!'*
As judges took place in his crew.

In Sinai, Moses' call came   144
From God, up the mountain – the same.
'Just keep all My laws
And My love will not pause.
You'll always be precious, by name!'

'To Me, you're a kingdom of priests   145
A nation that's holy. Like yeasts
Work wonders in flour,
All must come clean, this hour!' –
God spoke like *an MC* at feasts!

'These are the laws you must keep: 146
Put God first. Images heap
In a pile. But God's name
You must never defame.
And take a day off for a sleep!'

'Give honour to mum and to dad,   147
And don't murder folk, 'cos that's bad!
Adultery's wrong,
So is stealing, along
With saying your neighbour's a cad!'

'You have all you need in this life,   148
So don't covet anyone's wife –
Nor animals, spouse,
Or possessions, or house!
Bad habits cut down with a knife!'

'So long as we know where we stand,'   149
Said God, as he took Moses' hand,
'We'll get along fine –
Israelites, yours and Mine!
My blessings will shower on the land!'

'My rules are quite simple, you see 150
We'll get on forever, if we
Keep what we've agreed.
Then I promise your seed
Will flourish as sand by the sea!'

'In My ways, all folk should behave, 151
From birthday-time, right to the grave.
On festival days
Give Me praise upon praise,
And obey commandments I gave.'

Three feasts in the year were the rule, 152
Unleavened bread, Harvest – it's cool –
And Ingathering,
These became just the thing
They used year by year, as their tool.

'There's one thing more for you to do 153
At sacrifice-time, I want you
To sprinkle the blood
On the people, like mud,
As Covenant-trust we renew!'

'The next job for you is to make 154
The Ark of the Covenant. Take
The best things there are
From nearby and afar –
It must be superb, for My sake!'

'Ark's guardians must be appointed! 155
With holy oil, now be anointed.
The priests will then bear
Our God's Ark everywhere,
So Israel will not be disjointed.'

Aaron, meanwhile, had a thought   156
Of jazzing-up Israel with sport.
A calf made of gold
Would be fine to behold!
But would it be right? Did he ought?

Then Moses was fiercely enraged   157
With wickedness Aaron had staged.
He called folk together
To question them whether
On God's side their names should be paged?

Their dancing around golden calf   158
Made Moses say, *'I'll break in half*
The tablets of stone!
Let no Israelite moan!'
He banged on the ground with his staff!

'Sooner or later,' God said,   159
'You'll have your own land, and be fed
With milk and with honey,
It's really quite funny!
Ex-Egypt, forty years, instead!'

'Show me Your glory, I pray'   160
Said Moses to God, late one day.
'You can't glimpse my face,
But my back parts will race
Past you, Moses. Ready? Then stay!'

Next morning, up Sinai marched   161
Old Moses, his lips pretty parched!
'I'll write them again!'
Said God, *'My way, you'll gain*
Commandments, Mark 2, ironed and starched!'

His face shone, as if well sun-burned   162
From seeing God. Moses returned
And started again
All the people to train
In *God's* ways – the ones he had learned.

The Covenant-Ark needed men   163
All well-trained and loyal, so then
The rituals seen
Were well-done, smart and clean –
And plain in the Israelites' den.

The third book of Moses spells out   164
What Israel's religion's about.
The rules were so clear
No law-keeper need fear.
It organised all without doubt!

These sensible laws for your good.   165
Concern sacrifice, gifts, and food.
So if you behave
By the rules Moses gave,
You'll live as God said that you should.

The priests' job was keeping all sure   166
The nation was constantly pure.
What God had in mind
Was so well underlined,
There was nothing priests could not cure!

Vengeance, a dark dirty word   167
Is banned. So are grudges – you heard!
Give neighbours such love
And be blessed from Above –
For *I* am the Lord. *I'm* your God!

In Numbers, recorded as stated,
The Twelve Tribes of Israel rated
Their weakness and strength,
And their territory's length
For posterity – even though dated!

168

At meeting tent, soldiers fell-in!
You couldn't be heard for the din –
But Moses spoke loudly
And so very proudly –
He hoped they would take it all in!

169

Men twenty years old, who could fight,
Were numbered as warriors. Right!
Six-hundred-and-three-
Thousand-five-fifty. *'We*
Shall guard Israel's camp day and night!'

170

The vow of a Nazirite meant
That hair should be long. The intent –
Of not drinking wine
Or lush grapes from the vine –
To keep him God's special servant.

171

'The Lord bless you, Israel, and keep you!
The Lord make his face to shine on you!
The Lord lift up his
Countenance on you! This
Will give you His peace. Israel, it's true!'

172

Levites, at fifty, retire.
Their priestly work has to expire.
But ministering still
For their God, yes, it will
Be spiritually part of their fire.

173

NUMBERS 10: 1–11

The priests, who were all Aaron's sons   174
Blew trumpet sounds, signalling ones
Which sounded alarm,
Or just gave Israel calm.
At festivals, they blew great guns!

NUMBERS 10: 33–36

Wherever they travelled, in front   175
The Ark of the Covenant went.
It was covered by cloud
And no man was allowed
To touch it, unless it was meant.

NUMBERS 11: 1–9

'We reckon that Egypt was good   176
With free fish, and cucumbers! Food
Like garlic and leeks
Which we ain't had for weeks!
And melons – not manna for pud!'

NUMBERS 11: 10–22

God then sent them quails as they'd asked.   177
So easy for God, multitasked!
'For a month at the first
Eat them up till you burst –
Till quails through your noses have passed!'

NUMBERS 11: 31–35

Such food made the people go crazy   178
With orgy of lust, things went hazy.
A lot of them died
When God's word was defied –
They buried them under the daisy!

NUMBERS 12: 1–3

To Moses, the meekest of men,   179
God suddenly spoke there and then:
'You, only, have seen
Where My presence has been.
But for others, just visions, I ken!'

From each tribe of Israel, a guy   180
Was sent out by Moses, to spy
Out Canaan's land
Which God promised to hand
To them one day! God doesn't lie!

NUMBERS 14

The chaps started grumbling a lot: 181
'We had better times – (than we've got
Now) – in Egypt, as slaves!
Let's go back through the waves!'
But Moses and Aaron said, *'Not!'*

NUMBERS 16

Ringleaders, Dathan, Abiram,   182
Were scolded by Moses. *'Let's fire 'em!'*
At which came a 'quake
That devoured them! *'We'll make*
Them sorry the people once hired 'em!'

NUMBERS 17

Up sleeve Moses had one more trick.   183
Each tribe had to plant its own stick
In the ground. It would grow
If God wanted it so.
And Levi's one blossomed right quick!

NUMBERS 18: 21–24

'Give God ten-per-cent as your due'   184
Said Moses, *'And then it will do*
As payment for work
By the Levites. Don't lurk
Near the Meeting Tent curtains – yes, you!'

NUMBERS 19

He issued lots more regulations   185
For hygiene, and healthy relations.
'Make sure you keep clean!
Wash your hands, when you've been!'
And that's how they maintained their stations.

NUMBERS 21

The people, all bitten by snakes,   186
Said sorry. *'Just do what it takes!'* –
They begged. Moses made
A brass snake, and he laid
It on a big pole. *'Ditch the fakes!'*

NUMBERS 22

As Balaam rode his faithful ass,   187
'I'll face these guys at mountain pass!'
'I'm stopping right now!' –
Said the ass – *'and here's how!'*
Made Balaam reverse pretty fast!

NUMBERS 25

In order to keep the tribes pure   188
Rough justice prevailed, to be sure.
Phineas's spear
Killed a man and his dear –
Bad luck! An expedient cure!

NUMBERS 26

A roll-call was taken that day   189
And six-hundred-thousand said *'Yea!'*
'The land you will take
By proportion. You'll make
A nation for Me,' God said. *'Aye!'*

NUMBERS 27

'Choose somebody spiritual, one   190
Like Joshua, the son of Nun.
It's he who will lead us
And equally need us!
Together, will battles be won!'

NUMBERS 28–31

God gave Moses more rules again.   191
The Israelites learned them with pain.
'If you want to succeed
Then obey them, indeed!'
Said Moses, *'Then Canaan we'll gain!'*

This side of the Jordan, the land   192
Was good enough, and in their hand.
Said Moses, *'We oughta*
Cross o'er Jordan's water! –
Just so you all know where you stand!'

Despite some of their tittle-tattle   193
The Israelites focussed on battle.
'It's ours for the taking!'
Cried Moses, awaking
'So let's herd them up just like cattle!'

In Deuteronomy we see   194
Encouragement, for all to be
True, to God the Lord,
And to give God their word –
From now and to eternity.

The military campaign began,   195
And orders were sent to each clan
To pass by in peace,
Or to battle. Then cease.
'Our goal is to conquer Canaan!'

Moses strove hard to exhort   196
The strong men of Israel, who fought
With an eye on their sword,
And an eye on God's word,
In *this* way were victories bought!

The Lord made his Covenant stand.   197
All people here should understand
'His commandments – all ten
Should be learned and done! Then
God's blessings will rest in our hand'.

DEUTERONOMY 6

'O Israel, hear this,' – Moses cried,　　　　198
'Our God is one God. We have tried
To love God – that's right,
With heart, soul, and with might!
So all can say that we've complied!'

DEUTERONOMY 7

'Wherever you come across falsehood　　　　199
In worship, these idols are no good!
So break them all down
Never mind if they frown!
Just worship the one God as you should!'

DEUTERONOMY 8

'But when you become pretty rich　　　　200
Don't take all the credit, but ditch
Your pride in the bin!
It was God helped you win
Your wealth, and your health, without hitch!'

DEUTERONOMY 10: 12

'What God requires of you all here:　　　　201
Just follow his ways, and revere
Him, with heart and soul.
Give Him all – yes the whole –
Your love and devotion. That clear?'

DEUTERONOMY 12–26

The next fourteen chapters are Law,　　　　202
To know right from wrong, as before.
For instance, *'Don't eat*
Certain species of meat –
You'll bring Israel's reign to the floor!'

DEUTERONOMY 15

'Make sure that you look after all　　　　203
Who on bad times so harshly fall –
The poor and the weak,
And those who can't speak
For themselves – fat, thin, short, or tall!'

'Justice must always be done   204
And seen to work fairly. It's fun
When all play the game.
Keep the rules, and God's Name
Will go round the world, Number One!'

'A man who has sinned really badly   205
Will hang on a tree, rather sadly.
But take him down, men,
Before sunset – and then
Get him buried. That done – go gladly!'

'At harvest-time, make sure your best   206
Is given to God. It's a test
To judge your devotion.
So set things in motion
Right now, while your life still has zest!'

This chapter is all about curses,   207
For folk – who do wrong – lie in hearses!
'Just make sure that you
Do what God wants you to –
And then you won't need the wet-nurses!'

'So yet again comes the reminder   208
To keep faith with God. He'll be kinder
If you keep your word
And be true to your Lord –
This Pact is a man-and-God binder!'

Here Moses breaks out into song,   209
And does so – for he hasn't long!
He finally dies
In a grave the right size.
Don't know *where!* If you *do*, you're *wrong!*

JOSHUA 1

The Lord said to Joshua, *'Rise,*   210
And with Moses dead, just be wise!
Be strong as you go,
Cross the Jordan's full flow!
And spy out Canaan for size!'

JOSHUA 2: 1–14

Young Rahab lived by the town wall   211
At Jericho. Before nightfall
Came two Jewish spies.
'Shield us! Nobody dies
Here! Know our protection's for all!'

JOSHUA 2: 15–24

Escape was not easy, but she –   212
Red rope from her window, you see –
Let both spies get down
Out of Jericho town.
They, true to their word, let her be!

JOSHUA 3

Said Joshua, *'Follow the Ark,*   213
At Jordan's banks you'll need to park.'
No sooner arrived
There, the waters contrived
To allow them to cross before dark!

JOSHUA 5

Once over the Jordan, they go   214
In battle to win Jericho.
But God said, *'Your feet*
Must be bare, as is meet
When standing on holy ground!' So!

JOSHUA 6: 1–19

The priests with their trumpets and Ark   215
Round Jericho's walls sounded. *'Hark!'*
Said all the town people
When walls rocked, as steeple
In gales. Dogs then started to bark!

They marched seven days round the walls,   216
And cheered, blowing their trumpet-calls!
The people went hoarse
With their shouting, of course,
Till Bang! Crash! All Jericho falls!

JOSHUA 7

Some looting took place in the city   217
Of Ai, and it was a pity.
'It's just got to stop!'
Joshua said, *'And I'll cop*
All looters with death – stoned, and gritty!'

JOSHUA 10

The battles raged on, and they won,   218
As Joshua looked at the sun
And moon. They stood still.
But the battle raged till
The Israelites' warfare was done.

JOSHUA 14: 6–15

At eighty-five, Caleb said *'I*   219
Am strong as I ever was. My
Inheritance, Hebron,
Was Moses' gift – and on
My God I will always rely!'

JOSHUA 24: 17

The conquest of Canaan progressed   220
As Israelite soldiers confessed
That what they'd achieved
Was because they believed
In God. Their Pact – put to the test!

JUDGES 1

With Joshua dead, Israel sought   221
To elect a leader who fought
With God on his side –
Where the enemy died,
But Israelite casualties, nought!

Jael, the same – Heber's wife   222
Decided against use of knife.
With tent-peg in head
She killed Sisera dead!
So ended a chapter of strife!

JUDGES 5

Deborah sang praise, for God   223
Delivered them all on the nod!
She summed-up the war
In a few lines or more,
With forty years' peace on their tod!

JUDGES 7: 1-4

This is where Gideon came in.   224
The odds were against him. *'Begin*
To choose some sound men
Who are trustworthy, then
I'll lead you,' said God, *'and you'll win!'*

JUDGES 7: 5-7

Some lay down their weapons to lap   225
The water up. It was a trap!
But, weapons kept ready,
Some drank, cupped-hands steady –
Three hundred best soldiers on tap!

JUDGES 7: 8-18

Each vessel concealed a lit torch,   226
And Gideon ordered them, *'March!*
At the trumpet-blow
Break the vessels, and so
Wreak havoc on enemy's patch!'

JUDGES 7: 19-25

'The sword of the Lord!' they all cried   227
'Of Gideon, too!' – Foe defied!
Their trumpets they blew!
Such a hullabaloo!
As God spread their victory wide!

No sooner had Gideon died   228
When Israel denounced God, and cried
'We want orgies now!
Long live Baal! That's how
We want to enjoy life inside!'

Abimalech approached a tower,   229
'I'll burn it down within the hour!'
As these words he said
A millstone hit his head,
And pretty well killed him. Poor flower!

He didn't want people to know   230
A *woman* had beaten him. So
He begged to be slain
By his own sword. The pain
Was less than the shame of her blow!

Filled with the Spirit, he vowed   231
'I, Jephtha, say all this aloud:
If God's on my side
Then we all shall abide
In peace!' And to God's law he bowed!

To stop infiltration, a check   232
Was how to pronounce *'Sh.'* Oh heck!
Not *'Sibboleth'* pure,
But it's *'Shibboleth!'* – sure –
The password a spy might well wreck!

Here, Samson comes onto the scene.   233
The Spirit of God in him. Keen
To show off his strength
A young lion, full length
He conquered. *'It's nothing, I ween!'*

JUDGES 14: 7-9

So Samson walked back at his ease,   234
But came across hundreds of bees!
Inside lion's body
They swarmed, and yet oddly
From strong came forth sweetness! Yes, please!

JUDGES 15: 3-5

Samson wreaked havoc one night –   235
Caught three hundred foxes. Alight
He turned them into
Philistines' wheat field! Coo!
And gave all a jolly great fright!

JUDGES 15: 9-15

The Philistines camped near a pass   236
Where Samson met them, but alas –
He killed them, killed all
Quite a thousand men fall
By his weapon: a jawbone of ass!

JUDGES 16: 1-4

The Gazites then hatched up a plot.   237
'Next morning, at dawn, he'll be got.'
But Sam broke in two
The doors, posts, and, coo –
Like matchwood, he destroyed the lot!

JUDGES 16: 4-9

The Philistines tested Sam out.   238
With ropes, they secured him up. *'Lout!*
They jeered at him. Then
He burst free, yet again!
His strength legendary, no doubt!

JUDGES 16: 10-14

Delilah tried using her charm   239
This Samson chap's strong in the arm!
'How are you so strong,
Big chap? Now, come along –
I promise to do you no harm!'

'OK!' Sam said, *'Tie me up tight*
And I'll be your slave every night!'
But this was a tease –
She was weak at the knees
When Samson broke loose! What a sight!

JUDGES 16: 13

'Just tie me up tight by my hair,'
Said Samson. *'Is that pretty fair?'*
Delilah stood back
When the ropes snapped. Bang! Crack!
'You'll not find my weakness. So there!'

JUDGES 16: 21–29

The Philistines gouged out Sam's eyes.
Then, shaved by Delilah, the cries
Came as he pushed hard
On the pillars, like lard
In his hands, they gave way. Surprise!

JUDGES 16: 30–31

Three thousand had come for some sport
To see Samson's strength. But he caught
Them all, as he died –
See the pillars collide!
He slew more in death than he fought!

RUTH 1

Our Ruth was a Moabitess,
At Bethlehem, her new address.
She went out to glean
In the wheat fields. *'I've seen*
The man to be mine, if God bless!'

RUTH 2

'To Boaz, I want to be wed,'
Said Ruth, hoping he would be led
In her sure direction.
With eagle detection
Invited her, *'Glean here!'* he said.

240

241

242

243

244

245

> She snuggled-up with him that night,   246
> But he was not sure it was right.
> So, later next day,
> He did pay his way –
> His troth, Boaz to Ruth did plight!

RUTH 4

> It means that the family tree   247
> Of David, through Jesse, will be.
> Jesse's father – oh joy! –
> Came through Ruth's baby boy!
> The Jews' Royal Line, don't you see!

1 SAMUEL 1

> Elkanah and Hannah – though old   248
> Produced baby Samuel, we're told.
> He was *'Asked of the Lord.'*
> And they went overboard,
> Excited, enlarging their fold!

1 SAMUEL 2-3

> In song Hannah burst out! – His birth   249
> For her – was like no one's on earth!
> So precious was he.
> *'In God's service he'll be!'*
> And as Eli's mate, caused him mirth.

1 SAMUEL 2: 22-26

> Now Eli was well-on in years   250
> When rumours came into his ears.
> *'Your sons, we have found,*
> *With the girls sleep around!'* –
> And that increased Eli's worst fears!

1 SAMUEL 3: 1-5

> Eli was once sound asleep   251
> When Samuel heard his name bleep.
> *'You called me?'* Sam said
> *'What! Asleep in my bed?*
> *Just go back and keep counting sheep!'*

'*I'm here, Lord!*' – Sam said it again.
So Eli said, '*Keep saying then:*
'*Speak Lord, for I'm here!*
I'm Your servant!' – *and hear*
What the Lord has to say. It's so plain!'

252

1 SAMUEL 4

The Philistines captured the prize –
The Israelite Ark. They told wise
Old Eli, but he
Being ninety-eight, see –
Of shock died in front of their eyes.

253

1 SAMUEL 6

In those seven months such harm fell
On Philistines, Dagon, as well!
They sent it back nice
With gold tumours, gold mice,
With jewels and gold! Ain't that swell!

254

1 SAMUEL 7

In Kiriath-Jearim, it stood
For twenty years, just as it should.
At Mizpah, Sam prayed
That all Israel had made
A promise to turn to God. Good!

255

1 SAMUEL 8

The people nagged Sam day and night
'*We want a king! We think it's right!*'
But Samuel warned
'*That day has not yet dawned.*'
But put it to God – yes, that night!

256

1 SAMUEL 9-10

God answered Sam's prayer pretty fast,
For Saul arrived. '*He's here at last!*'
Anointed with oil
Saul became King and all –
The Lord's will on him had been cast!

257

He called all the tribes to meet there.   258
'You wanted a King! – Well, I'm here!'
The people went mad!
'He's the first King we've had!
God save him! God answered our prayer!'

Said Samuel, 'Come, let us go   259
To Gilgal, and there we shall show
The world we renew
The kingdom! O'er you
Saul's King! We rejoice! Ain't that so!

This Jon, of King Saul, the young son   260
Succeeded in battle, and won.
But angered his dad
'He must die! Yes, my lad!'
The people's great hero – this one!

At Bethlehem, David was found   261
When Samuel, family around
Anointed this lad.
'You'll be King!' That's not bad!
God's Spirit in him did abound!

Quite clearly, a man's outward show   262
Is what people look at. But no!
It matters much more
What his *heart* is all for!
The Lord looks at *that,* don't you know!

Saul felt rather down in the dumps   263
God's anger with him was like mumps!
When David arrived,
Played his harp, Saul revived –
No more experienced the humps!

The Philistines had a huge son –
Goliath, their bold champion.
He challenged Israel:
'Will no one there avail
To fight me?' Thus Gol thought he'd won!

264

Saul thought that he'd done the right thing
In kitting-out David. *'I'll bring*
My armour for you
To wear.' 'But it won't do' –
Said David, *'I'll just use my sling!'*

265

So David, the youngest of three
Accepted his challenge. And he
With sling aimed at forehead
Just killed the guy stone dead.
Beheaded Gol, for all to see!

266

David and Jonathan, they were
Such friends, they were soul-mates! Yes, Sir!
But Saul wasn't pleased
When the womenfolk wheezed
'David's far braver than you are!'

267

Saul's envy had boiled over when
He vowed to kill David. But then
He lunged with his spear
Twice, and so very near,
But God shielded David. Amen!

268

Saul set this young David a task
'One hundred Phili-skins, I ask –
And then you may marry
My daughter. Don't tarry!'
Dave scissored *two hundred* in cask!

269

They patched up bad feeling, but Saul 270
Tried hard to spear Dave in the hall.
He missed David's ear,
But Michal got to hear.
Dave fled through her window, down wall.

1 SAMUEL 21

Dave met the priest Ahimelech 271
Who said, *'Why alone? What the heck?*
Hey – don't eat that bread –
'Cos it's holy, I said!'
But Dave quaffed the lot down his neck!

1 SAMUEL 22: 1

So David escaped to a cave 272
The one of Adullam, and gave
Four hundred men
Good advice, there and then,
And became their leader. How brave!

1 SAMUEL 25

Dave wedded this young Abigail, 273
Companion wife to young Michal,
Ahinoam she
Became wife number three –
No wonder Dave looked rather pale!

1 SAMUEL 28

At Shunem, the Philistines' pitch 274
Was too close for Saul. Then a witch
At Endor foresaw
That Saul's life was no more!
'Tomorrow, you'll die in the ditch!'

1 SAMUEL 31

Saul's fortunes, this time, all turned sour 275
'The witch forecast it's my last hour!'
He suicide faced,
Just to die undisgraced.
The Philistines won. What a shower!

2 SAMUEL 1

Dave heard about Saul's death, as well   276
As Jonathan's, whom he loved well.
He sang a lament
For his friend who had meant
Such love in his life – it was hell!

2 SAMUEL 3: 36

At Abner's death, David was shocked.   277
Alliance with him had been rocked.
Yet the people approved
All Dave did, and they loved
Him, and to King David they flocked!

2 SAMUEL 5: 1–10

So David was now truly King.   278
All Israel, his subjects. *'I sing*
Jerusalem – thou
Art my home – and from now
The City of David's the thing!'

2 SAMUEL 6: 1–10

The Ark was the centre of dance   279
And music, a festival trance.
Poor Uzzah died there
As he touched it. Unfair –
For his oxen had stumbled just once!

2 SAMUEL 6: 11–19

For three months, the Ark rested still   280
At Obed-Edom's, yes, until
One day David said
That the Ark must instead
Be housed on Jerusalem's hill!

2 SAMUEL 9

He – Mephibosheth – was the son   281
Of Jonathan, he was the one
Whom David invited
So very excited –
But lame in both feet. Not much fun!

2 SAMUEL 10

Dave showed Hanun some deep contrition 282
Sent servants on a nice peace mission.
But they greatly feared
When he shaved half their beard,
Cut clothes in two. What a condition!

2 SAMUEL 11

Now David had earmarked a beauty, 283
Bath-sheba was his *cutie-cutie!*
He fixed it so plain
That Uriah was slain –
Her husband. She's now *David's* booty!

2 SAMUEL 12: 1–14

Nathan met David one fine day, 284
Told-off in no uncertain way!
'This baby will die
But you really must try –
Behave as God wants you. OK!'

2 SAMUEL 12: 24–31

So sorry was Dave, but contrite 285
He comforted Bath-sheba. *'Might*
We try once again?
Shall we name him? Like when?'
'Er – Solomon sounds about right!'

2 SAMUEL 13

David's son, Ammon, tricked Tamar 286
His sister. He – bad evil schemer –
Seduced her to bed,
But got slain. So it's said –
Their father put out a disclaimer!

2 SAMUEL 13

Absalom – he was their dad – 287
Just ran off with all he had.
King David was grieving
At both his sons leaving.
Small comfort, now Ammon was dead!

The crunch came when Absalom strove 288
To fight dad in battle. He drove
Right into an oak,
But got hanged! His last croak –
As his mule ran on up the grove.

Four Philistine soldiers, at Gath – 289
Six fingers, six toes one man hath –
Like giants, so tall
Each one slain, died. Thus all
Of Israel could get back its breath!

Old David waxed lyrical too – 290
And praised God for everything. *'You*
Delivered us all –
Saved Israel! I call
All people to join me. Thank You!'

These were David's last words in verse, 291
When things there went from bad to worse.
A pestilence great
Plagued the people – but wait!
He paid for the peace through his purse!

The days came, as David got old 292
His body felt more of the cold.
A girl, Abishag,
Warmed him up. *'Lass, I sag –*
I realise I'm losing my hold!'

David then called Bath-sheba near – 293
'I'm naming your son king, my dear!'
He said, *'Go tell Zadok*
And Nathan, the old crock –
That Solomon's next-in-line here!'

So Solomon saddled his mule   294
And came to them. *'Son – you're God's tool!'*
Said David. *'You're king
From now on – please sing!'*
Anointed by Zadok. That's cool!

So David instructed his son   295
In all regal things that were done.
And when David died
He was buried inside
Jerusalem's city. *Grave One.*

Then Adonijah, Sol's young bro   296
Asked Bath-sheba: *'Mummy, please go
And beg him to bless
As my wife, Abi-S!'*
But Sol said, *'No! Kill him! The foe!'*

Now, Solomon said in a dream   297
'I'm nothing like David!' A gleam
Came into his eye
When God said, *'By and by
You'll be strong, rich, wise. Stay abeam!'*

Two mums each had babies all right,   298
But one baby died in the night.
The first mum infers
That the live one is hers –
The other mum started a fight!

These mums tested Solomon's wares   299
They each claimed the baby was theirs.
'Then cut him in two!'
King Sol said, *'And then you
Will know who's the true mum! Who dares!'*

At that stage, the real mum cried out –
'Don't kill my son!' – she had to shout
To make King Sol see
And realise it was she
Who was the true mum, without doubt!

300

1 KINGS 4

God blessed him with wisdom so wise
That Solomon's fame reached the skies –
His proverbs and songs –
Almost endless! In throngs
People came to see him – a prize!

301

1 KINGS 5–7

The first thing Sol said they would do
To honour God, *'We'll build Jeru-*
Salem the finest
Temple! – Yes, we build best!
The world will come here for the view!'

302

1 KINGS 8: 12–21

They then brought the Ark up as well.
It had its own place, it was swell!
The tablets of stone
Moses brought down alone
Inside it. Such glory – priests fell!

303

1 KINGS 8: 22–30

Solomon with all his might
Prayed hard to God. *'In Your sight*
Let this temple be
Holy always, for thee,
And we'll praise You here, day and night!'

304

1 KINGS 8: 54–66

The temple now built, Sol spoke loud
'All Israel will praise God, I vowed!
We'll have a great feast,
Fourteen days at the least –
And party till late, with a crowd!'

305

It's not every day you can say 306
'The Queen of Sheba came today!'
But Sol gave her all
Her desire – what a ball –
And answered her questions! Hooray!

King Sol spent a lot of his 'dough' 307
On cleaning the temple up, so
It really looked swell,
And God liked it as well!
Such grand ideas! What a great show!

King Sol rather *spread it around,* 308
A thousand strange women he found.
Forgetting his vow
To the true God – he's now
For pagan gods, stuck in the ground!

Some rivalry threatened his reign – 309
Gave Solomon problems again.
It was over quite soon
But he died close on noon.
In Jerus'lem's grave he was lain.

The kingdom divided in two. 310
'King Jeroboam, we're with you!' –
Said those in the city
Jerusalem pretty –
For some, Rehoboam would do!

Jerry did naughty things then – 311
Made two golden calves, and said *'Men,*
You'll now worship these,
We can do as we please!'
At Bethel, and Dan, once again!

Came one day, from Judah, a man 312
Who challenged his evil ways. *'Can*
You be so disloyal
To God? Then the oil –
Anointing you king – never ran!'

This challenge made King Jerry think. 313
'It's true. I've done wrong! At the brink
Of things going awry
I'll repent 'ere I die!'
But meant it not. We saw him wink!

In fact, Jerry sinned all the more, 314
His household, rotten to the core.
With drink and with feast
He anointed as priest
Whomever he came across. Cor!

King Jerry persuaded his wife 315
To disguise herself, for the life
Of Abijah now
Was in peril, but wow!
Despite intrigue, son died. Such strife!

Although Jerry's sinning was sad, 316
Bro Rehoboam was as bad!
In fact, it was worse
Far too bad for this verse –
And Reho was buried with dad!

Abijam now wore the crown 317
And ruled in Jerusalem town.
But he soon died too –
It must surely be true –
As Asa the new king sat down.

So, various kings reigned. In turn 318
Each died, and was buried. We learn
That kings, bad or good,
In Jerusalem, should
Be judged for their deeds. Some would burn!

1 KINGS 17

Elijah the Tishbite came by 319
And lodged with a widow nearby.
Her food kept on growing,
Her son healed. *'Worth knowing –*
This prophet of God is some guy!'

1 KINGS 18: 17–21

Elijah, now at Mount Carmel, 320
Met prophets, the ones of Baal.
'A contest we'll set
To see whose God will get
These bonfires alight. Baal's – you'll fail!'

1 KINGS 18: 22–39

The Baal chaps tried hard all day 321
No fire from their gods came their way.
Despite drenched with water –
Alight El's one caught-a,
And Elijah's God won. Hooray!

1 KINGS 19

Elijah in cave refuge took 322
And faced wind and earthquake that shook
The ground round him there,
Also fire. *'Be aware'* –
'I'm God!' said a still small voice. *'Look!'*

1 KINGS 21

So, Jezebel played dirty tricks on 323
Poor Naboth. *'The blighter – I'll fix un!'*
She said, and wrote lies
To her Ahab's surprise –
And Naboth was killed. What a vixen!

A faithful young prophet was he.   324
'Samaria, I say you'll see
God's wrath on all them
As in Jerusalem!'
Micaiah: Eighth century BC.

1 KINGS 22: 29-40

King Ahab was hit. Arrow's point   325
Sunk into him just where the joint
Of his armour was weak.
'With my last breath, I speak:
'My son Ahaziah anoint!'

2 KINGS 1

King A'ziah had drunk too much wine   326
And fell through the window – a sign
He'd lived his life wrong
In God's sight. Before long
He died – as Elijah said! Fine!

2 KINGS 2: 7-8

Elijah took his coat, and hit   327
The river Jordan, and then it
Divided in two
As the prophet passed through
And so did Elisha! That's it!

2 KINGS 2: 9-13

Elisha said, *'I'd like to see*   328
At least twice your spirit on me!'
Then a chariot of fire
Whisked Elijah much higher
To heaven. Yes – *that's* where he'll be!

2 KINGS 2: 23-35

Elisha was off to Bethel.   329
When children there started to yell
'Hi, baldy!' they said –
Then two bears killed them dead –
All forty-two children! Well, well!

At Shunem, in her B & B,   330
Elisha asked, *'All this for me?'*
'A stool, table, bed,
And a candlestick!' said
Mine hostess, *'That's all you'll need, see!'*

2 KINGS 5: 1-12

Leprous, captain Naaman refused   331
To wash in the Jordan. Confused –
'The Damascus rivers
Just give me the shivers!
So what should I do?' Naaman mused.

2 KINGS 5: 13-14

'If one day I'd asked you to do   332
Some great deed, then come on – would you
Have done it?' *'Of course!'*
Naaman ordered his horse.
In Jordan, seven dips cured him, too!

2 KINGS 6: 24-30

The famine had reached a high peak   333
When two mums agreed that this week
They'd both eat a son.
So next day they ate one –
But Mum-2 backed-out, with a shriek!

2 KINGS 9

When King Jehu came to Jezreel,   334
She shouted abuse – Jezebel.
He said, *'Throw her down!'*
Her blood splattered the town,
Bits and pieces – all they could feel!

2 KINGS 10: 1-28

King Jehu demolished the lot –   335
Supporters of Ahab. He got
Rid of Baal pagans –
Like meat is to vegans!
Thus Israel returned to God. What!

Kept Jehu – the calves made of gold   336
At Bethel and Dan, as of old.
He paid for it, though,
Shunning God, they say so –
For twenty-eight years, then – stone cold!

The pattern for page after page   337
Shows kings doing things in their age
Like serving the Lord
Or not heeding His word –
Yet all achieved death as their wage!

The King of Assyria came   338
And defamed the Israelites' name.
Deported, they grew
Even worse than they knew,
And God got fed up with them. Shame!

With Josiah King, a change came.   339
He worshipped God, adored His name.
In a temple spring-clean –
'Look what I've found!' He'd seen
The Book of The Law. Very same!

He read it from cover to cover   340
And said it again, and then over
Again. *'Yes, one knows*
What the Covenant shows –
Let's do it, Israel, to recover!'

All pagan things Josiah heaved –   341
The idols, and cloth women weaved.
He dumped all the junk
Like a zealous young monk –
All purged for their good, he believed!

2 KINGS 23: 21-23

Josiah, Israelite King,   342
Commanded the people this thing:
'You must keep Passover
It's something that never
Must lapse. It's a serious thing!'

2 KINGS 23: 21-28

So, then King Josiah restored   343
The Passover feast, much ignored
For dozens of years.
Unique king, it appears –
Unusually true to his Lord!

2 KINGS 24

Nebuchadnezzar appeared   344
And deported Israel. They feared
They'd never return.
From Babylon. *'Burn*
The temple down!' King Nebbie said!

1 CHRONICLES 1-8

It seemed like a good idea then   345
To list all the Israelite men
And women, q.v.
Israelite family tree,
In eight lengthy chapters. Amen!

1 CHRONICLES 9-29

This book summarises events   346
From the days Israel lived in tents
To King David's death,
Right up to his last breath.
Of history, tries to make sense.

1 CHRONICLES 29: 11-14

Yours, Lord are the greatness, the powers,   347
Victory, glory, all hours,
With majesty too.
All the earth worships You,
All we have, You gave us. It is Yours.

2 CHRONICLES 1-36

This all starts with Solomon's reign
Repeats Israel's history again.
It ends with good news:
Persian King Cyrus' views:
'Return to Jerus'lem's domain!'

348

2 CHRONICLES 5: 13-14

The trumpets and cymbals both raised,
With singers too, their voices praised.
For the glory of God
Filled the house. So much cloud,
The priests could not stand. Truly dazed!

349

EZRA 1

King Cyrus was stirred by the Lord
'Return Israel's people!' His word
He kept. Gave back freely
What Nebbie had really
Just stolen, and taken on board.

350

EZRA 3: 1-9

Once back in Jerusalem they
Began to put straight all affray.
The workmen strove hard
Day and night in the yard.
In two years, were well on their way.

351

EZRA 3: 10-13

A shout went up there on the day
When foundation stone – so they say
For the temple was laid.
People wept – it relayed
So loud – they were heard miles away!

352

EZRA 6

Their enemies, sick to the core
Learned soon of the temple restore.
The whole thing exceeded
The size that was needed
When Solomon built his, before!

353

A problem concerning those who
Had foreigners married. *'Hey, you
Must give up your wives
If you value your lives!
No more foreign wives, from hereto!'*

354

Nehemiah was the one
Artaxerxes trusted. *'You, son
Must go back home now.
Build the walls up! And bow!'*
Jerusalem's glory begun!

355

Neh spent three days scouring the city.
Such devastation! What a pity!
Encouraged, they vowed
To rebuild and be proud
Of their work. That's the nitty-gritty!

356

Some people opposed what they did.
So it became urgent to rid
Themselves of the trouble.
They worked themselves double
With guards there, while the workers hid.

357

There's always someone on the fiddle,
And Neh spotted this. *'It's a riddle'*
He said, *'why you charge
Extortionately large
Fees for your work! Now restore it all!'*

358

A list was made up of those who
Returned to Jerusalem to
Begin all again
And forget all the pain
Of Exile in Babylon. Phew!

359

NEHEMIAH 8

Ezra again read the law 360
In front of the people, before
They forgot the ways
Of the Lord all their days! –
Those present bowed low to adore.

NEHEMIAH 9

The people agreed to take note 361
Of what they should do. Learned by rote
The rituals they
Should observe day by day –
And *no* more put God to the vote!

NEHEMIAH 10

Reminded of what Moses said 362
Was what Israel's people heard read.
It made sense to all
To live up to God's call,
And that way, their path would be led.

NEHEMIAH 11

To live in the city, they cast 363
By lots, amongst them, and they passed
All these good ideas
As God's will for the years
Ahead. They blessed all, first and last.

NEHEMIAH 13

It still needed work to be done 364
To get all the people as one
To observe the law.
And for every small flaw
Neh cracked the whip. *That* was no fun!

ESTHER 1: 1–11

Ahasuerus, yes, the king 365
Put on a great feast. Just the thing!
From India to
Ethiopia too
His empire extended. Ding ding!

ESTHER 1: 12–22

She blotted her copybook, sadly –   366
Queen Vashti refused rather badly
To attend the feast.
So the king dumped her – beast –
Then looked for another queen, gladly!

ESTHER 2: 1–16

It so happened there was a girl   367
Who caught king's attention. A twirl
Was all that was needed
To ensure he heeded
Her beauty. He'd found a real pearl!

ESTHER 2: 17–23

He loved Esther more than the rest   368
And made her his queen. *'She's the best!'*
Said happy King A.
But it wasn't his day –
Her family put him to the test!

ESTHER 9

The secret of Esther came out   369
That she was Jewess, no doubt!
But Haman's vile plot
Was discovered. She got
The answer: *'All Jews' foes – wipe out!'*

JOB 1: 1–5

This Job was a rather nice chap –   370
All luxury fell in his lap!
But Satan devised
Tests that were well-disguised –
Where Job might well give God the zap!

JOB 1: 6–19

A messenger came with bad news: 371
*'Your family is dead, and the mews
Are full of dead cattle!
It's likely to rattle
The most righteous man in his shoes!'*

But Job took it all on the chin.   372
He worshipped God, yet did not sin.
So Satan came running
With far greater cunning.
More tests were about to begin.

Job came out in boils everywhere,   373
The thing that might make a man swear!
But sitting in ashes
Job scraped at his rashes,
And spent a week pulling his hair.

Eventually, Job spoke his mind   374
And nearly cracked-up. But behind
Him, each day, there stood
His friends there, who were good
At comforting him. They were kind.

Eliphaz, Bildad, and Zophar   375
Kept visiting Job, the old gopher.
But what came across
Was that God was the Boss,
And Job never doubted His favour.

He wasn't convinced that what they   376
Told him was a help, come what may.
But Job knew that his
Own Redeemer still lives,
And that he'll stand at The Last Day!

Job makes many clever remarks   377
Convinced that God loves him, he harks
To what God says here:
'I heard God with my ear
But now, I can see him!' he barks!

Eventually, God blessed his life   378
And Job died in happiness. Strife
Had not got him down.
'I will never disown
My God!' So he'd said to his wife!

PSALM 1

The man who delights in the Lord   379
Shall be like a tree grown abroad.
Its leaves will not wither,
Nor will the man dither –
For God leads the way with His Word.

PSALM 2

The nations rise up and fall down,   380
Their greatness is not all their own.
But those who trust God
Will be blessed, though His rod
Occasionally causes a frown!

PSALM 3

Despite all the problems around,   381
It's God's words that always abound.
He shields you – yes you!
If you trust Him, it's true!
He blesses you! That's what we've found!

PSALM 4

At night, I will lie down in peace   382
Assured that God's love will not cease!
God answers my prayer
For I know that He's there.
In God, my trust's on the increase!

PSALM 5

Lead me, O Lord, to do right,   383
And make Your way plain in my sight.
For all who trust You,
Should rejoice as they do
Your will, Lord. There's no need to fight!

PSALM 6

Have mercy upon me, O Lord   384
And guide me, but not with Your sword!
My life is so bad
I become really sad
But try to keep faith with Your word!

PSALM 7

In You, Lord, do I put my trust!   385
I beg You to save me! I must
Not stray off Your path
Neither invite Your wrath!
I'll praise You forever, or rust!

PSALM 8

How excellent, Lord, is Your Name!   386
The universe echoes Your fame!
From the weakest small child
To the power of the wild –
The whole earth proclaims You the same!

PSALM 9

I thank You Lord, with my whole heart,   387
To praise You forever's my part!
The nations that shun You
You'll judge. And it's not new –
They are but men, so that's a start!

PSALM 10

The wicked man says there's no God!   388
He can't save himself on his tod!
Arise, Lord, and care
For the poor here and there.
Let wickedness rot in its pod!

PSALM 11

The Lord loves the upright man well,   389
The wicked can all burn in hell!
But righteousness brings
The way that He wants things
To be. That's the lesson to sell!

PSALM 12

It sometimes seems there's no one left   390
Who's godly. The world seems bereft
Of true faithful people
From temple to steeple
In this world's loom, from warp to weft.

PSALM 13

You won't forget me, Lord, forever?   391
Our enemies reckon You'll sever
Your love from us here.
They rejoice at our fear!
But I'll not stop praising You! Never!

PSALM 14

The fool says there's no God. That's fact!   392
From heaven, the Lord thought, 'React!'
'Is anyone here
Who fears God? The idea
Is far from our Covenant-Pact!'

PSALM 15

Lord, who is to dwell in Your tent?   393
Your holy hill? Only one sent
To live a pure life,
With his children and wife.
Whoever does this is a gent!

PSALM 16

I trust You Lord. Keep me that way.   394
Preserve me, Lord – I'm here to stay!
But those who desert You
Are Godless, and hurt You,
But You are my Compass all day!

PSALM 17

Don't let me slip down as I go,   395
Protect me, and be with me so.
Your wings' shadow hide me.
Let no lion chide me,
And I'll look for You, right – You know!

PSALM 18

My strength is in You, Lord – it's true! 396
Amaze me by all that You do!
This earth's myriad facets
Are some of Your assets –
If only the Godless ones knew!

PSALM 19

The heavens declare all God's glory, 397
And so does the earth. It's a story
That needs to be told
To all folk, young and old,
Much sweeter than honeycomb could be!

PSALM 20

When times are bad, the Lord still hears you, 398
And helps you, when you feel He nears you!
Some folk trust in horses,
In chariots, and forces –
Not us! Your name shows we revere You!

PSALM 21

When the king trusts in God, that's good! 399
You give him his heart's desire. Should
His enemies fight him,
Your hand will requite him,
And we'll sing Your praise! Yes, we would!

PSALM 22

My God, have You forsaken me? 400
It seems I'm abandoned – yes, me!
I'll still sing Your praise
For the rest of my days!
My family and I – we are *for* Thee!

PSALM 23

The Lord is my shepherd. He leads me. 401
Beside the still waters He feeds me.
I walk without fear.
Rod and staff show He's near!
The feast, at His table, soon will be!

PSALM 24

Who shall ascend the Lord's hill? 402
With clean hands, pure heart, then he will
Find gates open wide.
Which king goes right inside?
King of glory! The Lord of hosts still!

PSALM 25

I lift up my soul unto Thee! 403
My foes are no problem to me!
My past life, forgive,
In Your way I will live!
I trust You lots, Lord – don't You see!

PSALM 26

O Lord, be my Judge. You can see 404
My trust has been always in Thee!
Wherever I've been
I have washed myself clean,
To proclaim the way You lead me!

PSALM 27

The Lord is my strength, and my light, 405
And salvation. When foes in sight
Encompass me round,
I just long to be found
With You. Don't forsake me! That's right!

PSALM 28

O Lord, hear my cry when I call 406
And hold me up. Lord, lest I fall.
Give those who are evil
Reward from the devil!
For joy, my heart dances! A ball!

PSALM 29

Give God what He's worth! Give the lot! 407
His power is amazing. He's got
The world in His hands,
Mightiness in all lands!
His blessing of peace comes soon! What!

PSALM 30

You finally rescued my soul
But sometimes, I doubted Your rôle!
When things went so wrong,
I called You, loud and long.
But now, Lord, You've made my life whole!

408

PSALM 31

I trust You, Lord! – I know You'll never
Forsake me, and I shall be ever
So grateful in praise,
Not deterred by the ways
Of the wicked, for their lives You'll sever!

409

PSALM 32

I confess, my life has not been,
Lord, up to Your standards. I've seen
What happens to men
Who sin so much. But then,
I'm going to live Your way! I'm keen!

410

PSALM 33

Rejoice, and sing praises with lute
And harp, and with ten strings, to boot!
The strength of a horse
Will not save me, of course –
But we trust You, Lord! Yes, You're cute!

411

PSALM 34

O taste, and see, just how the Lord is
So gracious to those who take orders
From God, not from men
Who are fickle. But then
You'll take us with You. All aboard! Yes!

412

PSALM 35

O God, confound those who do harm!
Cause their way of life to disarm!
So long as they live
Lord, Your vengeance will give
Them their due reward in their palm!

413

PSALM 36

The ways of the wicked are bad   414
So much, Lord, that they make You sad!
But in Your true light
We'll all see what is right,
By giving up evil! – You're glad!

PSALM 37

Fret not yourself for all those who   415
Are ungodly – evil ones, too,
Whose ways are so bad
It's amazing they had
Such choice, to choose evil, or You!

PSALM 38

My health really has got me down   416
There's no good in me, on my own.
So come to me, quick
Lord, for I'm very sick!
You're God of my salvation!

PSALM 39

Lord, let me know when I shall die,   417
Lord, let me recover, so I
May be strong again,
And praise You! Yes! Amen!
At least, Lord, let me have a try!

PSALM 40

I sing with a new song today!   418
You're great, Lord! Hip, hip, hip, hooray!
Whoever deserves me
Lord, always preserve me!
But don't take too long! Help me! Hey!

PSALM 41

Whoever looks after the needy   419
You'll bless, Lord, and hope that it's speedy!
When I'm down in the dumps
Sure Lord, You'll man the pumps!
You'll help Lord! I hope I'm not greedy!

PSALM 42

My soul longs for You, like the hart　　　　420
Desires to drink water. Apart
From You, Lord, I fail
But with You, Lord, I sail
Above waves and storms! – I take heart!

PSALM 43

Defend me, O God – You're so strong　　　　421
Your light and Your truth – these I long
For, in Your holy house.
I've a heavy heart. Douse
My sadness! With harp, praise in song!

PSALM 44

Again, Lord, we pray You: defend　　　　422
Us now, and when we reach the end
Of life as we know it.
You'll *be* there! You'll show it!
Arise, Lord, and help us amend!

PSALM 45

The king's coronation is grand,　　　　423
Magnificent, best in the land!
The splendour is there,
While enhancing the fair,
With gladness and joy hand in hand!

PSALM 46

Our strength and our hope, when in trouble　　　　424
Is in God, when seas rage and bubble.
He makes wars to cease
And He brings about peace!
Be still, then. God saves you from rubble!

PSALM 47

At the trumpet's sound, God goes up.　　　　425
A merry noise makes us all clap!
For God is the King
Over all the earth. Sing
His praises! Just like a young pup!

PSALM 48

Our God is so great, in the city 426
Of Sion, so proclaim this ditty:
Our God is the King
Of the universe! Sing
His praises well! Don't make them bitty!

PSALM 49

Some think that their wealth gives them power 427
And never guess it's their last hour!
Don't think you're immortal –
We all pass death's portal!
You can't take wealth with you, my flower!

PSALM 50

The sacrifice God wants of you 428
Is not that of animals. True!
Just give God due praise
And still follow His ways,
And *that's* where salvation is due!

PSALM 51

Lord, please turn Your face from my sin, 429
And make me a clean heart within!
Don't go far away,
But be near me all day.
My lips will praise You, Lord! – You win!

PSALM 52

So, look at the man who thinks he 430
Can do without God. He will see
That his way of life
Just brings trouble and strife!
But I trust God's mercy. That's me!

PSALM 53

The fool says, *'There's no God!'* But then 431
That's typical thinking, of men!
We long for the day
When the Israelites say
'The Lord will deliver us!' – *When*?

PSALM 54

Please save me, O God, for the sake   432
Of Your name, and hear my prayer. Take
My heart, Lord, it's Yours!
I'll sing praise to Your doors!
Both when I'm asleep, and awake!

PSALM 55

When things get bad, Lord, You defend   433
Me. You have become a true friend!
I cast down my woes
At Your feet, Lord. It goes
To show how our lives can amend!

PSALM 56

Such troubles surround me all day,   434
But my trust in God's here to stay!
I'm not understood
By my enemies! Would
That they trusted God, like I say!

PSALM 57

My foes are like arrows and spears   435
With tongues like sharp swords! But God hears
My song – thanks and praise
Reach to heaven! I raise
My hands to You Lord! Wipe my tears!

PSALM 58

Lord, sometimes my thoughts are not nice.   436
Consume all my foes in a trice!
There's nothing too bad
For my enemy! Cad
That he is! Lord – he's full of vice!

PSALM 59

My foes grin like dogs, and they run   437
Around through the city. But one
Day, Lord, You'll give all
Of my foes, short or tall,
Their due reward! That should be fun!

PSALM 60

The nations around us are fearful, 438
But You help us not to be tearful!
You help us in trouble
And smite our foes double!
So make sure You give them a fist-full!

PSALM 61

O Lord, hear my prayer and my crying! 439
My heart is so heavy, I'm dying!
But under Your wing
I will praise You, and sing
Day by day! My foes need defying!

PSALM 62

God spoke once, and twice have I heard 440
That true power belongs to the Lord!
From Him comes my might
And my health, trust, and sight.
Let nothing deflect from Your word!

PSALM 63

I call upon You, Lord, at dawn 441
You've been with me since I was born!
By day and by night
I remember You – right?
I need You, Lord, from night till morn!

PSALM 64

For those who have nothing to do 442
With You, Lord, show them something to
Make them well-aware
That Your presence is there!
The man who is righteous trusts You!

PSALM 65

In Sion, O God, You are praised! 443
You hear all our prayers that are raised!
This intricate earth
You've made – gladness and mirth –
Even wheat fields laugh! We're amazed!

PSALM 66

The whole world, with joy, worships You! 444
You've always looked after us, too!
Lord, hear all my prayer,
And yes –You're always there
For me. I can't help praising You!

PSALM 67

Be merciful, God, and us bless! 445
We'll praise You, God! Let all confess
Your name on the earth.
Let the nations give birth
To Your way of living – no less!

PSALM 68

Let God arise – and let Him scatter 446
Our foes – so that, nothing will matter
But singing Your praise
For the rest of our days –
And worshipping You, as we natter!

PSALM 69

I'm frightened and stuck in the mire! 447
I'm weary of crying! Enquire
From God, who will save you!
It's your life He gave you!
Let heaven and earth form a choir!

PSALM 70

Deliver me, Lord, now, in haste! 448
And grind all my foes to a paste!
But those who seek You
Will find joy – yes, it's true!
But help me, Lord – let's say You raced!

PSALM 71

O Lord, let me not be confused! 449
My trust in You won't be abused!
And when I am old –
Please wait until I've told
The next generations Your news!

PSALM 72

When Israel's king trusts You, Lord 450
You'll bind nations up with a cord.
Let Israel be wealthy,
Its people all healthy,
And blessings from You will be heard!

PSALM 73

In Israel, God loves those who truly 451
Have clean hearts. But judgement comes duly
To those who are sinful –
They'll suffer a skinful
Of God's wrath. Let none be unruly!

PSALM 74

With You away, things have got worse 452
As if Israel's under a curse!
We've still got a Pact
And we know how to act
As You want, and You'll reimburse!

PSALM 75

Impressed by Your wonderful work 453
We realise that we mustn't shirk
From fighting the foe.
We want all men to know
That Israel's God is no quirk!

PSALM 76

In Israel God's name is well-known, 454
In Sion His tent and His throne.
We hold Him in awe
As we did years before.
He's wonderful, our God alone!

PSALM 77

I cry unto God. Does He hear me? 455
I wonder sometimes if He's near me?
His mercy – where is it?
We recall His visit
To Moses and Aaron by Red Sea!

PSALM 78

The history of Israel is fully   456
Recorded, but once more we duly
Read how God led us
With phenomenal fuss –
A powerful and patient God, truly!

PSALM 79

The heathen – they've entered the city –   457
Jerusalem's ruined! A pity!
The heathen with scorn
Ask us, *'Where's your God gone?'*
They'll reap their reward soon! That's witty!

PSALM 80

We must learn from lessons gone past   458
To trust God. He'll turn us at last
To follow His ways –
So as long as we praise
Him! We'll be whole then, and right fast!

PSALM 81

Sing merrily, make cheerful noise   459
With tabret, harp, lute, as our toys –
The trumpet as well –
With all these we will tell
How God once led Israel as boys!

PSALM 82

We look upon God as a judge   460
Defending the poor. He'll not budge
From justice for all.
Those who need Him may call,
And God will arise at a nudge!

PSALM 83

O God, keep not silence, but act   461
And let Israel's foes all be cracked!
Don't let them escape –
So they'll not make a jape
Of Your name – it's Israel You backed!

PSALM 84

My soul longs to enter Your courts –   462
Like birds, building nests, all have thoughts
Their young to protect.
I would rather expect
To be Your door-keeper, of sorts!

PSALM 85

Your graciousness pervades the land,   463
Lord. We are forgiven. You hand
Us righteousness, peace.
Truth and mercy increase,
You direct us all, as You planned!

PSALM 86

Among all the gods, there is no-one   464
Like You, Lord. We bow down. There is none
Other god who'll do
Great works, Lord, as You!
Your servant begs that mercy be done!

PSALM 87

Now, Sion's foundations are holy,   465
And God loves Jerusalem wholly!
The trumpets and singers
Eclipse Israel's slingers –
For all my fresh springs, Lord, are in Thee!

PSALM 88

I'm miserable, Lord, as You know,   466
And my life is all covered in woe!
In prison, I'm blind,
And my foes are behind
And around me – and I want to go!

PSALM 89

I sing of the Lord's kindness now   467
And glory in God's power, and how
His might is amazing
With nothing erasing
His record of victory. Wow!

PSALM 90

Our refuge, O Lord, in times past!　　　　468
Before all creation, You'd cast
Us into a mould.
And although we grow old
We know You'll be there at the last!

PSALM 91

Whoever dwells under God's care　　　　469
Need never fear anything there!
Whatever goes wrong
It'll not be for long –
And nothing is too hard to bear!

PSALM 92

At morning, it's time to sing praise　　　　470
By music accompanied. Raise
Upon God your sights
And you'll find He delights
In worship you've done all your days!

PSALM 93

The Lord is robed-up as a King　　　　471
Who made the whole world – every thing!
The waves of the sea
Still rage so horribly,
But holiness – God's peace will bring!

PSALM 94

O God, to whom vengeance belongs,　　　　472
How much more can we take of wrongs
The heathen devise?
They say, '*Tush! – no one spies
Us!*' Still – we praise God in our songs!

PSALM 95

O come, let us sing to the Lord　　　　473
And worship Him. We can afford
To give Him His due
As He makes all things new –
So – sing today with one accord!

PSALM 96

Just sing to the Lord a new song!　　　474
Sing praises to Him all day long!
In holiness' beauty
Make worship your duty!
Let all heathen know they are wrong!

PSALM 97

The power of the Lord is so vast!　　　475
His strength and His might He has cast
All over the place!
So let no tribe or race
Ignore Him! For He's first, and last!

PSALM 98

O sing a new song to the Lord　　　476
His victory came with His sword!
In music and hymn
Let the whole world praise Him,
And floods and hills clap Him aboard!

PSALM 99

The Lord sits on high in the heavens.　　　477
Israel, at sixes and sevens
Discovered His voice
In the cloud. They rejoice
In Sion, as His law now leavens.

PSALM 100

O be joyful, all lands – be glad　　　478
Be sure that the Lord, He is God!
He made us! He's pure!
Let His praises endure –
From father and son to granddad!

PSALM 101

Of Godliness, let me know more　　　479
And come to me, Lord, I implore!
But evil I'll shun,
Nor have wickedness – none!
I'll dwell with the faithful, for sure!

PSALM 102

O Lord, hear my crying, and prayer, 480
For I'm at rock bottom. Despair
Is my constant cry!
I'm not ready to die,
But You make the rules, and they're fair!

PSALM 103

My soul praises God. Like a dad 481
He takes care of us, though we're bad!
Our days, like the grass
Spring to life, then soon pass,
And we turn to dust. That's quite sad!

PSALM 104

God's power never ceases to thrill, 482
And birds, fish, and animals still
Are part of His plan.
From the dust, creates man!
To praise Him forever – I will!

PSALM 105

God's power was at maximum force 483
When Israel was set on its course
From Egypt. They went
Towards Canaan, and meant
To follow God's ways from the source!

PSALM 106

The people of Israel forgot 484
To follow their God. So they got
Themselves in such trouble
They had to pay double
For what they had done, and had not!

PSALM 107

In times of distress Israel's prayers 485
To God were like climbing steep stairs!
When God bailed them out
They took no time to shout
His praises. Then ditched Him for years!

PSALM 108

I'm ready, Lord, my heart is ready,   486
My faith in You grows deep and steady!
Your help in the past
Indicates it will last!
Our confidence makes us quite heady!

PSALM 109

Such wickedness round us is sadness,   487
And I don't approve of the badness
That goes on all round!
But as soon as they've found
Out the truth of You, Lord! *That's* gladness!

PSALM 110

King David was God's right-hand man,   488
But God's power was far greater than
One could have perceived
When David first believed
That he was a part of God's plan!

PSALM 111

The works of the Lord are so great,   489
And all His commandments relate
To His Pact between
God and man. They are seen
As wisdom begins in man's state!

PSALM 112

The man who does what God wants will   490
Be blessed in abundance, and still
Will fear nothing bad
For God's word he has had –
But those who are wicked, He'll kill!

PSALM 113

From sunrise to sunset we'll praise   491
The name of the Lord, and we'll raise
Him high o'er the heathen
His glory o'er heaven,
With families happy for days!

PSALM 114

When Israel fled Egypt's land 492
God parted the Red Sea – that and
The waters of Jordan,
Defeated their cordon,
And hills skipped like sheep, hand in hand.

PSALM 115

The heathen are at it again! 493
'So, where is your God?' their refrain.
But their gods are dead
From the feet to the head!
While we praise the Lord – they're a pain!

PSALM 116

It's so good when God hears our prayers, 494
It uplifts your soul, ends your cares!
I walk now with Him
And thank God I'm not dim!
In the Lord's house I mount the stairs!

PSALM 117

The nations should all join in praise, 495
The heathen should praise all their days!
God's kindness is there
More and more, yes, I swear!
The Lord's truth endures, and it stays!

PSALM 118

Those who fear the Lord, now confess 496
His mercy dispels strain and stress!
The builders erected
This stone once rejected –
He comes in God's name, and will bless!

PSALM 119: 1–8

Blessed are those who walk in 497
The way of the Lord, and don't sin!
With You, Lord, I gained
And my heart prays unfeigned –
You'll never forsake me! You win!

A young man cleans up his whole act   498
By keeping Your word, and Your Pact!
For what You command
Is so clear. Let it stand –
And *then* You will see him react!

Your statutes are all that we need   499
So open our eyes, that we heed
The words that You say
Which I keep day by day!
Your servant, Lord – yes Lord, indeed!

My soul is stuck fast to the dust,   500
And so I pray, Lord, that I must
Seek truth and be clean
So You'll know where I've been,
With no more deception, I trust!

O teach me to learn, Lord, to stay   501
In touch with Your laws day by day.
Make my eyes to see
Your laws, not vanity,
And quicken me, Lord, in Your way!

I long for Your mercy and love   502
O Lord, send it down from above.
I lift up my hands
To receive Your commands,
To walk in Your ways – but don't shove!

At night I have thought of Your name.   503
I sing it by day – just the same!
The ungodly, though
Frighten me, Lord, and so
I don't want to play in their game!

I promised to keep all Your law   504
O Lord, but at midnight I saw
That my life is lacking
So don't send me packing!
Your mercy is what I implore!

I haven't lived pure as the snow,   505
But now I love You, so I know
Your law is worth more,
And I've learned to adore
Your statutes, Lord. Ain't that just so!

Your hands, Lord, have fashioned and made me   506
But I need to learn more, Lord. Aid me!
Your judgements are right
And Your law – my delight!
The wicked will want to evade me!

My soul, Lord, longs for Your salvation.   507
I long for Your comfort. My station –
Like bottle in smoke.
Foes say, *'What a sad bloke!'*
What can I do for reparation?

Your word, Lord, endures there forever   508
In heaven. But Your word will never
Go far from my mind.
I'll not leave it behind,
Despite all my foes do. Whatever!

Lord, You know that I love Your law   509
I study it all day, and more!
Your laws make me wiser,
They're an appetiser –
Like honey gets stuck to my jaw!

Your word is a light for my feet,   510
A lantern, to light my paths. Greet
Me, Lord, in the dark
Where my enemies park
Their traps for me. Make them retreat!

I hate those who imagine evil,   511
Whose lives are controlled by the devil!
But 'stablish me fast
Lord, so I at the last
May stamp them out as a small weevil!

I deal with what's lawful and right,   512
But now it's affecting my sight!
I want to know more
Of Your law, but abhor
All false ways. Your law's a delight!

Your word gives such light to the simple,   513
It forms on my mouth like a dimple!
It makes my eyes cry
When bad people defy
Your laws, Lord. Such folk – a bad pimple!

Righteous are You, O Lord! Be near me!   514
My zeal, Lord, has even consumed me!
I feel of no worth
Amongst people on earth,
But I'll keep Your laws, and I'll fear Thee!

I call with my whole heart, Lord, You know   515
I try to do what I should, e'en so
At morning I cry
Out for You, Lord. Be nigh,
And may Your commandments in me grow!

Deliver from adversity,   516
Health is far from the ungodly!
I have many foes,
Lord, yet none of them knows
I'll never swerve from Your mercy!

PSALM 119: 161–168

Lord, princes without any cause   517
Have persecuted me. Your laws
I've loved. As for lies
Those I hate and despise!
I praise You each day! Yes, of course!

PSALM 119: 169–176

I beg You, Lord, deliver me   518
In order that Your praise should be
My song every day.
I've gone so far astray
Lord, like a lost sheep. Rescue me!

PSALM 120

I called on the Lord, and He heard me,   519
So troubled, what could He do for me?
If peace only came
When I mention its name!
My enemies just want to fight me!

PSALM 121

I lift up my eyes to the hills,   520
My help comes from God, despite ills.
While He keeps me safe
Sun and moon will not chafe.
My comings and goings God wills!

PSALM 122

I was glad when they said to me,   521
'Let's visit the Lords' house. Let's see
Jerusalem's peace!'
And there, I'll not cease
To *do* good, and *be* good. That's me!

PSALM 123

To thee, Lord, I lift up my eyes 522
Have mercy, for they all despise
Us. They are the wealthy,
And proud, but not healthy!
So Lord, we pray You – hear our cries!

PSALM 124

If Israel had not had the backing 523
Of God, we would not have sent packing
The soldiers of Pharaoh.
But we took the air – oh –
Like birds from the snare! It was cracking!

PSALM 125

Those folk, those whose trust is as solid 524
As Sion's mount – a fortress stolid –
Will stand fast forever.
The wicked will never
Prevent peace in Israel. They're horrid!

PSALM 126

When Israel's freedom emerged 525
We laughed, cried with joy, joy that surged
Like seeds in a field
Which developed a yield,
As reaper brought sheaves that converged!

PSALM 127

Unless it's the Lord God who builds it 526
The house will not last. Just believe it!
The kids you produce
Are like arrows shot loose,
And happy the man who won't doubt it!

PSALM 128

The chap who fears God will be blessed, and 527
He will eat the labours of his hand.
His wife like the vine
Will have kids, maybe nine!
Prosperity, and peace, in our land!

PSALM 129

Some problems arose in time past,   528
But God was there, from first to last.
Like grass they were treated,
But not one was greeted
With *'Good luck in God's name!'* Surpassed!

PSALM 130

Lord, out of the deep have I called Thee,   529
O Lord, hear my voice, I implore Thee.
My soul flees to You
Lord – just say that it's true –
Redeem Israel. End of story!

PSALM 131

I'm humble, Lord, with no proud looks.   530
I'm not a high-flyer with books.
My soul knows no other
Than child with his mother,
And Israel's caught fast on God's hooks!

PSALM 132

To God David once made a vow –   531
His children would keep *the Pact.* How?
In Sion, God's blesses
All David's successes
By clothing his foes with shame now!

PSALM 133

It's good, and it's joyful, to dwell   532
Together in unity! Well –
It's like the anointing
Of Aaron, God's blessing
On Hermon in Sion is swell!

PSALM 134

You servants of God, you who stand   533
At night, praising God, lift your hand
And praise Him again
All your life! It is plain
In Sion, God's blessing is grand!

PSALM 135

Keep praising the Lord – yes, the real One 534
Above other gods, not as was done
In Israel's past
Pagan gods cropped up fast –
As lifeless as those who designed 'un!

PSALM 136

Give thanks to The Lord, fail Him never, 535
His mercy endures – yes, forever!
The Exodus showed
How God's power really flowed,
Let no one from God Israel sever!

PSALM 137

By Babylon's waters, we wept 536
We hung up our harps, as we slept.
They said, *'Sing a song
Of Sion!'* It's so long
Since we left there. Songs were inept.

PSALM 138

My whole heart is so full of praise! 537
Your truth, love, and kindness amaze!
You hear when I call,
Pick me up when I fall.
You save me when trouble affrays!

PSALM 139

You know when I stand or sit down. 538
There's nowhere where You're not in town!
In heaven, You're there
As in depths of despair!
No foe competes with God's renown!

PSALM 140

The snares of the ungodly try 539
To trap me. O Lord, hear my cry!
You only avenge
All Your foes! And revenge
Is Yours. I'll still praise You on high!

PSALM 141

O Lord, keep me on the right track
And don't let me ever look back
On my evil ways.
Let my foes never raise
Their traps, Lord. Just give them the sack!

540

PSALM 142

My soul was in heaviness when
I cried to the Lord. Free me, then
I'll give thanks always
For the rest of my days –
And live as the most righteous men!

541

PSALM 143

I think of the past quite a lot,
And thank You for all that I got!
So teach me to do
All the things that please You!
My soul gasps, as if it's red hot!

542

PSALM 144

Defend me! In You, Lord, I trust!
My armour for battle won't rust
With You at my side!
I sing now – though I cried –
My friendship with You is a *must!*

543

PSALM 145

Let all speak of You, Lord, Your glory
And praise is a wonderful story!
We wait upon You
While You give us our due,
And scatter and rout the ungodly!

544

PSALM 146

As long as I live, I will sing
The praises of God. Everything
He does is so good –
Gives the hungry their food.
In Sion, our God shall be King!

545

PSALM 147

> God builds up, and heals. And He knows 546
> The names of the stars, and all grows
> In His plan made clear
> All things live for Him here –
> The animals, and belles and beaux!

PSALM 148

> The grandeur of God's world portrays 547
> His power, and fantastic ways!
> So all – young and old
> See the story unfold,
> And praise Him the rest of their days!

PSALM 149

> O sing a new song, Israel! 548
> Let children in Sion all tell
> The world of their joy –
> Every girl, every boy –
> With tabret and harp, dance as well!

PSALM 150

> God's holiness, greatness, and power 549
> We praise, with loud music, each hour!
> Harp, trumpet, and lute,
> Cymbals, dances, and flute!
> All who breathe – praise God, *our Papa!*

PROVERBS

> Though Solomon wrote a good many, 550
> The Proverbs emerged two-a-penny.
> They give good advice
> On what's nasty, or nice.
> Just learn some by heart, or not any!

PROVERBS 25: 11–12

> A word fitly spoken, we're told 551
> Is like lots of apples of gold
> In silvery baskets
> Like wisdom in caskets –
> So learn this before you get old!

PROVERBS 25: 21–22

If enemy's hungry, it pays 552
To feed him! If thirsty, amaze
Him by your kind acts,
Quick, before he reacts!
So heap coals of fire on his ways!

PROVERBS 30: 15–16

You never can satisfy these: 553
The grave, and the childless! One sees
That earth without water
Is to son and daughter
A problem – like fire in the trees!

PROVERBS 30: 24–28

Four things that show wisdom: in turn 554
The ants, and the rabbits both learn
To live on the land.
Locusts, lizards both stand
In hot places – and yet don't burn!

PROVERBS 31:10–31

A virtuous woman is rare. 555
To find one, where would you look – where?
But find one whose word
Shows that she loves the Lord
And no one will with her compare!

ECCLESIASTES 1: 2

'All vanity!' – that's what he said – 556
The Preacher's face grew rather red.
'There's nothing round here
Except vanity, dear!'
In which case, we should go to bed!

ECCLESIASTES 1: 15–18

The crooked thing can't be made straight. 557
In debt, there's not much to create!
In wisdom is grief.
And the man who's a thief
Will find just the same. Soon or late!

ECCLESIASTES 2: 18–19

I can't bear to think that my work
Is left for someone who will shirk.
If foolish or wise
Then he sees with his eyes
It's all *vanity* – no mean quirk!

558

ECCLESIASTES 3: 16–22

We know, whether good, whether bad,
That God judges us. We all had
The same love or lust,
And we all turn to dust!
It's all *vanity!* Sad or glad!

559

ECCLESIASTES 4: 9–12

Two chaps are far better than one,
In half the time get the job done!
With someone beside you
It's warm! Woe betide you
If you face a foe on your own!

560

ECCLESIASTES 9: 12

When fishes are caught in the net,
And birds in the snare, even yet
We can't know the day
When our life fades away.
If *that's* a surprise, then – get set!

561

ECCLESIASTES 12: 12

Of the making of books – no end.
And wisdom is learned, so amend
Your life while you may,
But don't read all the day –
Much study is wearisome, friend!

562

ECCLESIASTES 12: 14

This is our whole duty – we can
Fear God, and then work to His plan.
For God will judge all
That we do, so recall
That everything's *vanity,* man!

563

This – written by someone who knew   564
The tenderness Israel had, too –
The fighting and wars
Just showed *one* side. But pause
At *this* song of loveliness, do!

Whole chapters describe with affection   565
The beauty of each. In one section
Their love hits the heights!
They are smitten! The nights
And the days their lovesickness mention!

THE SONG OF SONGS 8: 6-7

On your heart, set my seal. Make me fit   566
As a seal on your arm. Quite a bit
Of life on this earth
Shows that love's strong as death!
Floods can neither quench love, nor drown it!

ISAIAH

Isaiah is in three parts, so   567
I mention it, just so you know!
(Perhaps this best-quoted
Book ought to be noted –
For Jesus Himself knew it! Oh!)

ISAIAH 1: 11-14

The Lord says, *'I've had quite enough*   568
Of animal sacrifice! Tough!
I want no more incense
So please make no pretence –
Just don't mix the smooth with the rough!'

ISAIAH 1: 18

'Come, reason together, my friends'   569
The Lord says. So let's make amends!
With scarlet sins, know
That they'll be white as snow!
Not red, but like wool, when sin ends!

ISAIAH 2: 4

When we walk the way that God wants,   570
The nations will find His peace blunts
Their swords into ploughs,
And for pruning the boughs
Their hooks will be what spears were once!

ISAIAH 2: 19

Some time in the future, there'll be   571
A Day of the Lord – just you see –
When men out of fear
Will hide there, and hide here –
From glory of His majesty!

ISAIAH 3: 16–26

When daughters of Zion are haughty   572
And mince around, ever so naughty –
God's judgement will come
And affect every home!
It's likely to be their last sortie!

ISAIAH 4–5

It's going to be terrible for   573
Some people, with such woes galore!
The sea will be roaring
With people imploring
The Lord to pass by their front door!

ISAIAH 6: 1–8

The year when King Uzziah died   574
I saw the Lord enthroned, and sighed
As seraphim lowly
Sang 'Holy – yes, holy –
The Lord of Hosts's holy!' they cried.

ISAIAH 6: 9–13

Go, tell all the people. They hear,   575
But understand not! – It's so clear
They see, but they don't!
In their hearts they just won't
Turn round, and be healed! Dear, oh dear!

ISAIAH 7: 14

A sign from the Lord Himself will 576
Tell you that a young girl – a thrill –
Will bring forth a son
And He's truly The One!
His name will be Immanuel!

ISAIAH 8: 14–15

The Lord is a sanctuary – true! 577
A stumbling block and snare, if you
Ignore His commands!
It's just what God demands!
But woe betide you till you do!

ISAIAH 9: 2, 6, & 7

The people who walked in the dark 578
Have seen a great light, and remark
That God's name is great!
A mere child will translate!
No end to His peacefulness – mark!

ISAIAH 11: 1–5

From Jesse's house a branch shall grow 579
With wisdom, and knowledge, you know,
With counsel and might
And the fear of God – right!
(It's *Jesus* he means!) There you go!

ISAIAH 11: 6–9

The wolf now at peace with the lamb 580
The leopard and kid – just like jam –
Will mingle together
With calf, lion – whatever –
A child leads the whole lot! Yes, Ma'am!

ISAIAH 25: 8–9

The Lord God will wipe away tears 581
And end the reproach of the years,
As He lifts up the veil
From the nations' travail,
'We've waited for this day, My dears!'

ISAIAH 28: 16

In Zion, the foundation stone 582
Becomes so important. There's none
So precious as that
Corner-stone! It's the mat
Upon which the nations' feet run!

ISAIAH 32: 15

In due time, the Spirit will pour 583
Upon us from on high – and more!
In the desert, springs fruit!
From the wilderness root
A forest shall grow up! Encore!

ISAIAH 35: 4–7

Your God will come one Day, and then 584
The blind will see, deaf will hear! Men
Will leap, though they're lame
And will sing the Lord's name!
And streams in the desert will run!

ISAIAH 35: 8–10

A highway called *'Holiness'* there 585
Will be, for the ransomed ones, where
No sadness or sorrow
But gladness! Tomorrow
Will be Zion's joy now – so rare!.

ISAIAH 40: 1–2

'Comfort my people, and speak,' 586
Says God, *'and please tell them this week*
Their warfare is over,
From sins now recover!
It's true, both for strong as for weak!'

ISAIAH 40: 3–8

A voice cries out, *'Make the way straight* 587
For God! Level mountains, and wait
To see God's true glory
And then tell the story
Because this comes from the Lord, mate!'

Tell Zion! Tell Judah! *'He'll come –*   **588**
The Lord God! The lambs in His arm
He'll so gently carry.
This shepherd won't tarry,
But he'll keep you safe from all harm!'

To whom will you liken God, then?   **589**
With what can you compare Him? *Men?*
With *idols of metal?*
With *workmen's fine fettle?*
You *can't* compare God! D'ya ken!

Those will – who upon the Lord wait –   **590**
Renew all their strength, and not faint!
Like eagles they'll fly,
Run, and not be weary!
They'll walk with God, at a fresh gait!

My Servant, in whom I delight   **591**
Shall be to the Gentiles a light!
He'll open blind eyes,
And in prison surprise
All, leading them out of their plight!

Drop down from above, from the skies   **592**
And let heavens open. Your eyes
Will openly see
Your salvation from me,
With righteousness too, as the prize!

I then gave my back to the smiters,   **593**
My cheeks to those there who were fighters,
Who plucked off my hair,
Spat at me without care,
And made me endure this! The blighters!

ISAIAH 52: 7

How beautiful there are the feet   594
Of those, who, with good tidings greet
All – nephew and niece –
And who publish such peace:
'Our God reigns in Zion! Let's meet!'

ISAIAH 53: 3–5

He was so despised and rejected   595
Of men, and by sorrows afflicted.
He was wounded for us –
Our iniquities, plus
By His healing stripes, we're affected.

ISAIAH 53: 7–9

Led like a young lamb, tied-up and penned, 596
In silence, no words there to defend –
For our sins He died,
And His grave was beside
Wicked men's. Innocent to the end!

ISAIAH 55: 6–12

So, while you can find the Lord, seek   597
Him! You'll be led forth with the peak
Of the mountains and hills
Which will break forth in thrills
Of singing, and clapping, all week!

ISAIAH 56: 5–8

My house shall be called *'House Of Prayer'* 598
For all nations. Everyone there –
The strangers as well
As yourselves, Israel –
Will worship the true God, all year!

ISAIAH 61: 1–2

God's Spirit is on me! Hooray!   599
I preach the good news, that I may
Uplift broken-hearted,
Free captives – once started,
The Year Of The Lord's here to stay!

JEREMIAH 1: 1–9

The child Jeremiah said, '*I*   600
Can't speak, Lord, in public!' 'But why?'
Said God, '*You will go,*
And what you'll need to know,
I'll tell you! – So go on, and try!'

JEREMIAH 5: 31–6: 14

False prophets in Israel mislead   601
The people, and wallow in greed!
They falsely cry, '*Peace!*'
Blatant lies, full of grease –
And nobody cares much, indeed!

JEREMIAH 11: 6–8

Young Jerry pitched into a few   602
Who centralised worship, but knew
That God wants the heart
For his law. Just a part
Of Jerus'lem's city won't do!

JEREMIAH 11: 18–23

Resistance to Jerry proved strong   603
With arguments frequent and long.
Jerusalem nobs
Said '*We'll all lose our jobs!*'
'*It's your fault!*' said Jerry – '*You're wrong!*'

JEREMIAH 20: 7–18

Poor Jerry became laughingstock   604
As folk came along just to mock
Him day after day
As they passed on their way.
'*Lord, why put my head on the block?*'

JEREMIAH 23: 5–8

The Lord said, '*One day soon, I'll raise*   605
Of David, a righteous branch. Gaze
On his wise, long reign
When all Israel will gain
Their own land!' Now *that's* worth some praise!

Sometimes, the prophets there would seem   606
To have special knowledge: *'I dream*
This, that, or the other!'
We have to ask whether
Their dreams are their own, or God's, scheme?

The picture of Zion's great fun –   607
When all Israel's tribes join as one,
And dance in the street –
Young and old, they all meet
In joy, now that sorrow's clean gone!

My Covenant's a Pact that will be   608
Engraved on your hearts, Israel! See –
I'll be your true God,
So you won't think it odd –
For you'll be My own people! Yippee!

O Lord, by Your power You made   609
Both heaven and earth. I'm afraid
I've got to admit
That Your power shows me it
Finds nothing that it can't pervade!

Once, Jehoiakim, Israel's king   610
Told Baruch to write up a thing
He later destroyed.
So Baruch, still employed
By Jerry, just wrote it again!

Poor Jerry was dumped in a pit,   611
When Ebedmelech said that it
Was wrong. *'Come here men*
We'll pull him out again!'
Such friends helped Jerry quite a bit!

In Zion sat Baruch, sat he   612
About year five-six-o BC.
He wrote Lamentations,
A sad tale of nations –
(Not by Jeremiah, maybe!)

It's quite chockablock with the woes   613
That Israel faced, against their foes.
He mourns for the Zion
He once knew, but iron
Is not quite like gold, and it shows!

LAMENTATIONS 1: 12

Is it nothing to you, who pass by?   614
Don't you ever sit down to ask why?
Is there any sorrow
Today or tomorrow
Like mine? Have I made God so angry?

EZEKIEL 1

Ezekiel slept on, and he dreamed   615
That Israel was not as it seemed.
His visions were stark
Like a storm in the dark,
All round him weird imagery teemed!

Some creatures with wings and strange face –   616
A man, eagle, ox, wheels that race,
And fire where they went!
What this dream could have meant
Was puzzling, like holes within lace!

EZEKIEL 2

The Spirit came into him finally,   617
Ezekiel realised eventually
That he was the one
God had picked to become
A prophet in Israel, convincingly.

The Spirit uplifted me, and 618
A rushing wind said, *'Understand*
In this place, the glory
Of the Lord! Your story
Will take you to a foreign land.'

To make the point, old Ezek lay 619
On left side for many a day.
And then on his right –
Forty days at the sight
Of Israel and Judah *mauvais!*

And then Ez cut some of his hair 620
And weighed it in three, then and there.
He burnt it to show
How the nation would go,
But no one much bothered to stare!

Not very long after, in Zion 621
The Spirit whisked me there to spy on
The evil being done
By almost every one –
Not quite the folks God could rely on!

In all this, God softened and said 622
'I'll give them a new heart! Instead
Of stone, let's have flesh
So that they walk afresh,
And I'll be their God till they're dead!'

Folk *are* being seduced by false words, 623
Proclaiming there's peace, when it's swords!
Don't paper the cracks
While they don't guard their backs,
Catastrophe's coming, you nerds!

EZEKIEL 34

'A shepherd,' the Lord said, *'I'll be*   624
And seek out my sheep – just you see!
In pastures so green
Is where My sheep have been,
And I'll care for them! They're with Me!'

EZEKIEL 37

A valley of bones, full, and dry,   625
But can these bones live? *'Let me try!'*
The Lord said, and blew
His breath over them – true –
Inspired with new life – they said, *'Hi!'*

EZEKIEL 37: 10–14

My Spirit inside you will show   626
New life, and in this you will go.
When you have your own land –
You must all understand
That I am your God. Fear no foe!

EZEKIEL 37: 27–28

The covenant God made forever   627
Was something Israel must not sever.
My sanctuary
Israel's centre, shows we –
You and I – will not part. That's never!

EZEKIEL 43

In vision, I'm now at the gate   628
Of eastern Jerusalem. Wait! –
The Spirit led me
With God's glory, to see
The Temple restored at some date.

DANIEL 1: 1–2

Nebuchadnezzar the king   629
Of Babylon formed a great ring
Around Zion's city
And said, *'What a pity! –*
To Babylon, now, you I bring!'

Neb wanted some bright young men who   630
Were skilful in knowledge. *'You'll do –*
Azariah and Daniel
Hananiah, Mishael.' –
Neb gave them new names, as you do!

So now, Belteshazzar was Dan,   631
And Az was Abednego, man!
And Han was called Shadrach
While Mishael was Meshach,
All part of old King Nebbie's plan!

King Neb set a task. His wise men   632
Must guess what he dreamed about, then
Tell him what it meant
Or their heads would be rent
From them! Oh – but they didna ken!

So Daniel prayed hard, and up came   633
Solution to old Nebbie's dream.
An image of gold
Just fell down, so we're told,
And into a mountain became!

Old Nebbie asked, *'What does this mean?'*   634
Then Daniel explained, *'It is seen*
That one Day, there'll be
God's great kingdom, you see,
Which never will end! Tell the queen!'

Neb promoted Dan straightaway,   635
And gave him the Governor's pay,
As he oversaw
All of Babylon, for
King Nebbie. And that made Dan's day!

DANIEL 3

An image of gold King Neb made 636
And said, *'When the music is played,*
All must bow down low!
If you don't, you will go
In furnace so fiery – you'll fade!'

DANIEL 3: 8–22

Inevitably, three refused 637
And so did a lot of the Jews.
So Neb chucked them in
To the furnace. A grin
Came over his face. *'I'm amused!'*

DANIEL 3: 23–30

But Shad, Mesh, and Abednego 638
From fire emerged unscathed. *'Hello!'*
Neb was so impressed
He said they were the best –
Promoted them all in a row!

DANIEL 4

More dreaming of grandeur Neb had, 639
Which Dan understood. He was glad –
So much so, that he
Led King Neb to agree
That Dan's God was best! *'Well done, lad!'*

DANIEL 5: 1–4

Belshazzar's feast – plenty of wine 640
And women, and song. By design
He used temple vessels –
(Such sacrilege hassles!) –
But thought, *'This is great! It's just fine!'*

DANIEL 5: 5–7

A moment came, somewhat sinister 641
When fingers wrote words on the plaster.
Bel came over faint,
'What do these letters paint?
Interpret these words for your master!'

Again, Daniel came to the rescue!   642
'You're weighed in the balances, but you
Are found sadly wanting!
Mene Tekel Upharsin:
Phew! Your kingdom is long overdue!'

That night King Belshazzar was slain!   643
So Darius assumed the reign.
'Put Dan to the test!'
He cried, *'and all the rest!*
In lions' den they will remain!'

No law of the Persians and Medes   644
Could ever be changed. So then pleads
Daniel to God. *'We need*
Your help to be freed!'
By lions unharmed, Dan succeeds!

Successful, Daniel made King Dar   645
Proclaim decree: *'Men near and far*
Will worship the true
God – that's Daniel's – who
Delivered him from lions' power!'

It was Dan's turn to dream, not the king's!   646
The first was a lion – yes – with wings,
The second a bear,
And a leopard was there,
And a beast, ten horns, man's eyes, and things!

In clouds, in the heavens, appeared   647
A son of man – widely revered –
The Ancient Of Days,
To whom all men give praise –
Whose kingdom forever endured!

Interpreting dreams wasn't easy   648
In fact, it made Dan feel quite queasy:
'Four kingdoms remain,
But the Most High will gain
Whole world – which for Him's easy peesy!'

This vision upset Dan a bit –   649
Unsure what he might make of it!
'This kingdom is given
To the saints in heaven
Who'll serve and obey, as is fit!'

A second dream Dan had, please note,   650
A ram charged a poor billy-goat!
The billy-goat won,
'Aha – now we'll have fun!'
Said Dan! This is then what he wrote:

Gabriel, the angel, made clear,   651
'Daniel, the ram – this one dear –
Represents all –
Medes and Persians will fall,
As Greece conquers everything here!'

So what Daniel dreamed as a piece   652
Came true. Persia yielded to Greece!
What seemed like a trick
This apocalyptic,
Summed-up Israel's yearning for peace!

Hosea had had a bad marriage.   653
His wife had gone off like a carriage!
As unfaithful wife
He compared Israel's life
As nation. Would this make God savage?

Despite being deserted by them
God said, *'It is true, there's no phlegm*
At all on My part –
But there's love in My heart!
Your wife should be prized like a gem!'

654

HOSEA 6: 6

To make the point, God said, *'Look – I*
Don't want sacrifice, but mercy!
To know God is more
Than burnt offerings, for
That's what sort of God I am! Hi!'

655

JOEL

The son of Pethuel, called Joel,
Had warnings for Israel. Well, well!
'The locusts will come!'
He said, *'and you'll be dumb*
If you don't repent quickly, Israel!'

656

JOEL 2: 1-2

'It's going to be horrible gloom
With clouds and thick darkness and doom!
For The Day of the Lord
Will arrive like a sword!
Prepare yourselves now! Flee to whom?'

657

JOEL 2: 12-14

The Lord says, *'Turn now, even now!*
Rend hearts, not your garments!' God's slow
To anger! But note
His compassionate vote
Is merciful, gracious! And how!

658

JOEL 2: 28-29

'My Spirit I'll pour out on all.
Your daughters and sons will enthral
In prophetic team,
While your old men will dream,
Your young men, with visions, will fall.'

659

'The sun shall turn dark, with a croak,   660
The moon to blood, with fire and smoke
Before The Day dawns,'
'It will be' – Joel warns –
'The time when God judges a bloke!'

'Let all men of war listen here.   661
Turn pruning-hook now into spear!
Beat ploughshares to swords
You must listen – My words
Says God – *'are the things you must fear!'*

A shepherd called Amos in Judah   662
Kept fig trees. He lived in Tekoah.
But God sent him north
Telling him, *'You speak forth*
Against Jeroboam, the rotter!'

King Jerry had set up an idol –   663
A golden calf. This was a trial
For Amos, so brave
Proclaimed that God would save
The righteous alone, not the vile!

The traders aren't good when they cheat!   664
Dishonesty is never sweet!
To sacrifice daily
But not repent, really –
A very strange use of raw meat!

The first chap in Testament Old   665
To write, was young Amos the bold.
The priest at Bethel
In the king's pay as well
Said, *'Quit, Amos, now you've been told!'*

In warning folk, Amos had meant
To steer Israel back to repent
Of evils they'd done,
Or they'd find – every one –
That God would be fierce in judgement!

666

AMOS 7: 7–8

The Lord, in a vision, showed me
A plumb line beside a wall. *'See
This line, Amos? It
Will test Israel. Sit
A moment. What will its fate be?'*

667

OBADIAH

In one chapter only, we see
Obadiah, steward was he.
As Jezebel raves,
He hid prophets in caves,
A hundred of whom he set free!

668

JONAH 1 :1–2

God contacted Jonah: *'Convey
My message at once! Nineveh
Is wicked. Don't moan –
You must go on your own!
Whatever you do, don't delay!'*

669

JONAH 1: 3

But Jonah had no plans in mind
To go there. Instead he would find
Excuses galore –
Visit some other shore,
And leave Nineveh well behind!

670

JONAH 1: 4 –15

A tempest blew up, and the ship
Fair broke into pieces. The trip
Was now a disaster.
*'We'll just have to cast ya
Right into the sea for a dip!'*

671

It happened that a great big fish   672
Was also en route to Tarshish.
It saw Jonah wallowing
And couldn't help swallowing
Him up! *'This is some tasty dish!'*

By night and by day Jonah prayed   673
To God. *'I'd much rather have stayed
On dry land,'* he said.
Three days after, it's said
The fish spewed him up! *May Day! Aid!*

A second time, God told him to   674
Go to Nineveh. *'Tell them, do –
Repent this same day
As there's no other way!'*
So Jonah obeyed this time. Phew!

The king and the people prayed hard,   675
And fasted, with Jonah on guard,
When God showed his pity
By sparing the city,
But Jonah had played his last card!

He sat 'neath a gourd in the shade   676
Which withered next day. A tirade
From Jonah came then
*'How could God forgive men
Whom Israel their enemy made?'*

So God had to teach Jonah quickly   677
A lesson that made him quite sickly.
*'It pays to show pity
E'en to a bad city!'*
Said God. Exit Jo, feeling prickly!

MICAH

To Micah, the Morashtite came 678
The word of the Lord, just the same
As that of Isaiah,
Of Amos, Hosea –
To Samaria – Jerus'lem.

Predicting that both places would 679
Be destroyed for what was not good –
Their bad evil ways
To the poor there, betrays
How badly their leaders had stood!

MICAH 6: 7-8

The Lord said, *'I'm fed up with rams* 680
As sacrifice, or babes in prams,
Or rivers of oil!
What I want from your soil
Is justice and mercy! Sirs! Ma'ams!'

NAHUM

From Nahum the Elkoshite, three 681
Short chapters contain prophecy.
About six-one-two
Nineveh – yes, it's true –
Was captured by Babylon, see!

NAHUM 2-3

Assyrian capital city 682
Yes, Nineveh, town without pity,
So cruel to those
Who were Nineveh's foes,
'You'll be destroyed!' was Nahum's ditty.

HABAKKUK

In Judah, Habakkuk thought hard 683
How God could use foes who were tarred
With wickedness such
As the Chaldaeans! Much
Distress caused to Israel! Some bard!

He prayed at great length, and with style,   684
To God. And his answer came while
He realised one Day
That all nations would pay –
As God judges all, good or vile!

ZEPHANIAH

Of Cushi, Zephaniah, son   685
Warned people in Judah to shun
Their idols and magic.
Their worship was tragic,
With God's laws infrequently done!

But those who came back to God would   686
Enjoy the future as they should!
The darkness and gloom
Would evaporate! Boom!
And life would be brighter, and good!

HAGGAI

In two chapters, Haggai's distaste   687
For those in Jerusalem who faced
Such comfort and ease
In their houses! *'But, please –*
Look hard at the temple – now disgraced!'

HAGGAI 2: 18

'Let's build it again, even better,'   688
Said Haggai, bold to the letter!
'The foundation stone
Has been laid. Now don't moan,
But – let's get it built!' A go-getter!

ZECHARIAH 1: 1–17

In five-twenty BC, the Jews   689
Returned to Jerusalem. *'Lose*
Heart? That you must not!'
Zech said, *'What we have got*
To do here is proclaim good news!'

He spent time encouraging men

To rebuild the temple and then
To start to be proud
Of what freedom allowed –
'A bright future follows! Amen!'

ZECHARIAH 9: 9

O daughter of Zion, rejoice!

Your king comes to you. He's your choice!
Though, riding so slowly
Upon an ass, lowly,
With salvation, justice, and poise!

ZECHARIAH 12: 10

'On David's house, and Zion's face.

I'll pour supplication and grace.
And those who pierced me
Will look closely, and be
As mourners who walk at slow pace.'

ZECHARIAH 13

In those days, the shepherd will flee

And sheep will be scattered, you'll see!
But one Day, you know
Living waters shall go
Out from Zion's city! Yippee!

MALACHI

Now, Malachi – that was his name

Means *'messenger.'* He would proclaim
The coming Messiah!
No message was higher,
And that was Mal's one claim to fame!

MALACHI 1: 11

From sunrise right up to sunset

God's name shall be great, even yet
Among Gentiles' land
In all places, where stand
The offerings of incense. He's great!

'My messenger prepares My way   696
But who here may abide The Day
He comes? Who shall stand
When with fire in his hand
He purifies silver? Who may?'

'Behold, I will send down to you   697
Elijah the prophet, he who
Will foretell The Day
Of the Lord, and hearts may
Turn to one another!' Tood'loo!

The Apocrypha

1 ESDRAS

Describing their history, the Jews

698

Returned from exile with the news:
'Darius the king
Will support rebuilding
Our temple – to give him his dues!'

1 ESDRAS 3

King Darius first posed a riddle

699

To bodyguards. Three, in the middle
Debated with king
'What's the strongest? What thing?
A puzzle, chaps!' Hey, diddle diddle!

The four options put to those men

700

Were wine, or the king, or women,
Or truth? What a choice!
But the king heard the voice
Of Zerubbabel once again.

'The answer is truth!' he replied!

701

'I really agree!' Darius sighed!
So, as you have won
The prize, you are the one
Who'll go back to Zion with pride!

'Go – rebuild your temple today!

702

And I'll help you do it! I'll pay
As much as it takes,
There are no higher stakes!
Let it be Jerusalem's Day!'

Events of their nation, this book 703
In summary form. Take a look!
From Exodus to
The Apocalypse, you
May read up what course history took!

TOBIT

In Tobit, the author writes on 704
Conditions in old Babylon.
The Jews there in exile
Were urged to be faithful
To God, Whom they rested upon!

He recommends a way of life 705
Encompassing virtue, not strife!
'It's good to give alms
As a habit. It charms
The needy, as well as your wife!'

Old Tobit went finally blind 706
But Raphael the angel, so kind
Helped cure him, we learn
And on Sarah's return
From a demon, in marriage they bind!

In chapter five, verse sixteen, we 707
Read he had a faithful doggy!
Its favourable mention
Is no mean invention –
Unique in the bible! Wow! Whee!

JUDITH

In Judith, a novel we find – 708
One of an historical kind.
The hatred comes through
Of the Gentiles – a Jew
Would try to rid them from his mind!

Its orthodox stance clearly shows   709
That faith in God overcomes woes.
But Nebuchadnezzar
Failed in his attempts there
To win Jews' support 'gainst his foes!

So Judith, a widow so young   710
And beautiful, sang them a song.
To God she gave praise
As she tried to erase
The Jews' fear of anyone strong.

THE REST OF ESTHER

Unique in the Bible, we read   711
No mention of God here! But heed
The Feast of Purim
Which to Jews meant a hymn
Delivering from death indeed!

THE WISDOM OF SOLOMON

An Alexandrian Jew wrote   712
This book, as if, by him of note –
King Solomon. But
The words that he put
Down here, were much later, I quote!

From virtuous living to the   713
Choice of friends, this book seems to be.
With practical details
On learning, it retails
The fear of the Lord, don't you see!

The fear of the Lord is the start   714
Of wisdom, which springs from the heart,
Or is it the head?
Like what Solomon said!
Just read it, to feel you take part!

Read Ecclesiasticus, when 715
You'll know all about famous men
Who strove after wisdom!
If only CD ROM
To them was available then!

So Wisdom, a female form takes – 716
A nice idea, yes, one that makes
A man pay attention!
For by her instruction
A man, who sleeps, finds he awakes!

It tells what will make a man glad 717
As well as what makes a man sad.
A woman or man
Who is bad in life can
Find some wise words here! Yes, by gad!

From chapter four-four he lists men 718
So famous in Israel! Then –
From Abraham to
BC one-thirty-two,
He shows wisdom's effects! Amen!

BARUCH

This book, at first sight by a Jew 719
Had Christian influence too –
Put in some years later
By a Greek translator –
Maybe not Baruch. Wonder *who?*

In chapter six, we have a letter 720
Which might have come very much better
From Jeremiah
Yes, the prophetic sire –
The one whose book's in the OT, Sir!

It harks back to when the Chaldaeans 721
Invaded Jerusalem, aeons
Ago! Yes, enquire –
They destroyed it with fire!
A sad time! Of praising, no paeans!

THE SONG OF THE THREE HOLY CHILDREN

In far greater detail, we see 722
The plight of those men, yes, all three
Who walked in the dire
Fiery furnace, the fire
Didn't touch them! As Daniel says, see!

In sixty-eight verses, we're told 723
Of those three, the ones who were bold
In facing disaster!
But praising their Master
They emerged unscathed! Pure as gold!

From verse thirty-five, comes the nicety – 724
Familiar song – *Benedicite!*
It prays that all things
Should praise God, and it sings
'His mercy endures for eternity!'

THE HISTORY OF SUSANNA

In sixty-four verses this lass – 725
Accused of a crime that was crass!
But Daniel's wisdom
Delivered this woman
From rumours that she'd *made a pass!*

It happened on one sunny day 726
That Susie went out to play
Naked, in her garden
Where, unseen by two men,
She started to wash herself. Hey!

Those two men approached her alone
And got her down there on her own.
'You lie with us here!
If not, we'll say we hear
That you planned it all, so don't moan!'

But Susie screamed with a loud voice!
Alerted the guards. *'What's the noise,*
Susannah?' She cried
'It's these men!' and replied –
'They threatened to rape me! The goys!'

At this Daniel came to the court
'I represent Susan! Her sort
Is innocent! You
Know that she's a good Jew!'
Death came to those two men they caught!

BEL AND THE DRAGON

Two stories attached to the text
Of the Book of Daniel. It vexed
Him about the lies
That were told. *'I despise*
All falsehood!' Dan said. What came next?

There was a huge image called Bel
Where people brought food – lovely smell!
Each day it appeared
That the food disappeared –
(The priests knew where to, very well!)

But folk thought that Bel always ate it
Till Dan said, *'Look – these priests, they get it!'*
Exposing their ruse
Became such headline news,
That Bel was destroyed, to Dan's credit!

The priests too, were put to death, and 733
Dan's fame spread throughout all the land!
The next story, though
Is a nasty one, so –
It might make your hair on end stand!

Derived from a Semitic myth 734
A dragon seized Dan in its teeth!
But Dan won king's vote
When he rammed down its throat
Some balls of fat, hair, and black pitch!

The people, enraged that he'd won 735
Persuaded the king, that for fun
Young Daniel should be
Caged with lions, not three
But seven! And so it was done!

But right in the nick of time, Dan 736
Was saved by Habakkuk, who ran
Amazingly too
From Judea! But you
Believe it or not – yes, you can!

THE PRAYER OF MANASSES

So, put into words, just as if he 737
Manasses, the king, wrote them. Did he?
This short book of prose
Is a prayer that goes
Quite movingly, to God Almighty!

The scene's set in Babylon where he 738
Was captive, in exile. So you see
That Israel's king
Manasses had to sing
God's praises, and yet ask God's mercy!

In roughly one-hundred BC   739
This book was compiled, so that we
May read what it seems
Like, beneath the regimes
Of Greek rule, for Jews like MacBee!

Antiochus Epiphanes,   740
Exterminates Jews there like fleas!
Obsessed with Greek culture
He swoops like a vulture
With Jerusalem on its knees!

1 MACCABEES 1: 20–24

The temple was first on his list.   741
He stole from it, and with his fist
In BC one-six-eight
He said, '*Exterminate*
All those Jews, who my rule resist!'

1 MACCABEES 2

The history of his deeds of evil   742
Are really quite unbelievable!
But young Mattathias
Had none of this bias
Towards pagan gods, or the devil!

1 MACCABEES 2: 15–22

One day, under pressure – '*Conform!*   743
Or you'll pay the price! – It's the norm!'
But Matty resisted
'*I won't!*' – he protested!
And so a rebellion did form!

1 MACCABEES 2: 23–26

One day, in the temple, Matt slew   744
A worshipper there, yes, a Jew –
Obeyed pagan orders,
In Israel's borders!
So Matt killed the officer, too!

On Matt's death, his son Judas rose –   745
As fearless, as the record shows.
In turn, came Jonathan
And then brother Simon –
A merciless lot, to their foes!

1 MACCABEES 6: 43-47

A strange tale of Eliazar: 746
He charged on an elephant. *'Aargh!'*
He said, as with fear
He lunged deep with his spear,
And killed the poor beast through its rear!

1 MACCABEES 16

But at the last they met their ends,   747
No more was Zion in their hands!
The Maccs' bold uprising
Was really surprising!
Greek rule now, once more, is what stands!

2 MACCABEES

The second war of Maccabees,   748
Was equally bold, if you please!
Now Antiochus
Has been slain, then for us
The temple's ours! Worship at ease!

Once more, subterfuge ruled the day   749
And intrigues increased all the way.
But the day came when
The Greeks Rule, OK! Then
Israel had no more to say!

One incident shows pain and stress   750
A woman endured. *'No? or Yes?'*
Her tormentors said –
'You'll bow low, or you're dead!' –
She'd not submit under duress!

To make her crack up, they killed seven 751
Sons in front of her, who were even
Scalped, and fried alive,
Butchered. She said, *'Look, I've*
A man's strength! I'll see you in heaven!'

And so it goes on to the last! 752
Some history of Israel is cast
Within the Apocrypha
So that we know of the
Problems and triumphs they passed!

The New Testament

MATTHEW 1

In Matthew, the family tree753
Shows Jesus was born Royalty!
Searched each generation
Of the Jewish nation –
From Abraham to 6BC.

MATTHEW 2: 1–2

Wise men from the east came to see754
Where King of the Jews was born. *'We*
Saw his star in the sky
And we're just passing by,
To worship Him. Where can He be?'

MATTHEW 2: 3–8

In Bethlehem, Judah, a son755
For Joseph and Mary – the One
Was born King of the Jews.
Then King Herod got news.
'Find this child!' Herod stormed. *'No King! None!'*

MATTHEW 2: 9–10

They followed the star all the way756
To Bethlehem, where the child lay
In the darkness that night.
When they saw him, the sight
Was one of exceeding great joy!

MATTHEW 2: 11

They offered their gifts then and there:757
Gold, frankincense, myrrh they prepare
For the King of the Jews.
Tinged with sadness, the news –
The suffering Jesus would bear!

MATTHEW 2: 12

The wise men used wisdom that night –
Avoided King Herod like blight!
They travelled a way
Which was safer. So they
Returned home, after seeing *The Light!*

758

MATTHEW 2: 13–14

But Joseph was warned in a dream
To escape to Egypt. *'This team
Has saved our child's life!'*
Joseph said to his wife.
Two years safety, at last, it would seem.

759

MATTHEW 2: 16

King Herod was not very pleased
When given the slip. His diseased
Old body was racked
With revenge. *'I want hacked
To death infants aged two!'* He wheezed.

760

MATTHEW 2: 19–23

News now came that Herod was dead.
'It's safe to go back!' Joseph said.
To Galilee truly
They travelled, and duly
Made home there, to Nazareth led.

761

MATTHEW 3: 1–16

Baptising in Jordan, John came –
'Repent, for the Kingdom!' – his claim.
'Not worthy – no, never!'
Dipped Jesus in river.
His cousin was never the same!

762

MATTHEW 3: 16–17

The moment of truth came about
When John lifted Jesus right out
Of the water. *'My Son'* –
Said a voice – *'is the one
In whom I am pleased! Without doubt!'*

763

MATTHEW 4: 1–9

The time came for Jesus to think   764
Of his future. The devil would wink
If he turned stones to bread,
Ruled the world, or be led
To jump off the temple's high brink.

MATTHEW 4: 10–11

The scriptures are so very clear   765
'Don't tempt God!' it says, 'So I fear
Your efforts are wasted!
Now Satan – you're pasted!
Don't ever come tempting me here!'

MATTHEW 4: 12–13

At this stage, the Lord moved his base   766
From Nazareth to seaside place.
'Capernaum's home
For me now! Let us roam
Through Galilee, preaching apace!'

MATTHEW 4: 18–25

He gathered a small group of men   767
Who would learn from him everything, then
Be his right-hand people
From temple to steeple
And spread the Good News. *'Master, when?'*

MATTHEW 5, 6, & 7

'Just wait till I've taught you, my friends'   768
Said Jesus, *'and my Spirit sends*
You power from on high
Makes you bolder, and I
Will be Shepherd! And that's how God tends!'

MATTHEW 5: 2–12

He taught the crowds on a small hill   769
About blessings, and what's God's will.
'Be good to each other,
And do love your brother!
Be kind and be helpful. Don't kill!'

Jesus taught *'The poor will be blessed,*   770
The bereaved, the meek, and the rest,
Those who hunger and thirst
And make peace, will be first
In the Kingdom of God. They'll be best!'

MATTHEW 5: 13

'Of the earth,' Jesus taught,' *you're the salt.*   771
If its taste ever comes to a halt,
Then cast it on ground
Where men's feet pound around.
If salt's no good, it's its own fault!

MATTHEW 5: 14–16

'It's no good concealing a light –   772
It's got to be useful at night!
Its purpose, you see
Is to shine out, like Me –
And end what is evil. All right?'

MATTHEW 6: 1–8

'Don't show off in public. Your alms   773
Are 'tween you and God! It just harms
Whatever you do
If it's not really true
To your calling. So watch the alarms!'

MATTHEW 6: 9–15

'Just pray to the Father. Give praise.   774
His Kingdom will come. Yes it stays!
Ask daily for bread,
Forgive wrongs, and instead
Make up with each other! It pays!'

MATTHEW 6: 19–21

Don't lay up your treasures on earth,   775
Where rust, yes, and moths have their berth;
But store it in heaven,
And no thief will even
Try adding your wealth to his girth!

MATTHEW 6: 25–34

> *'Don't worry about what you'll wear*   776
> *Or eat, 'cos you've nothing to fear.*
> *The lilies don't wither,*
> *The birds don't starve either!*
> *And God provides everything here!'*

MATTHEW 7: 15–20

> *'Beware of the people who dress*   777
> *As wolves in sheep's clothing, no less!*
> *Know folk by their fruits!*
> *Bad roots bring bad shoots!*
> *Make sure that your lives aren't a mess!'*

MATTHEW 7: 21

> Not everyone who says, 'Lord, Lord,'   778
> Shall enter the Kingdom of God.
> When you do God's will
> You'll ensure that you still
> Are welcome in heaven. 'Come aboard!'

MATTHEW 7: 24–27

> *'Make sure that you build upon rock.*   779
> *Your building must stand every knock!*
> *If you build it on sand*
> *Not a chance it will stand –*
> *But collapse! And your neighbours will mock!'*

MATTHEW 7: 28–29

> Jesus taught with authority, not   780
> As one of the scribes, who had got
> His learning from books
> Such were nothing but crooks –
> And their teaching was all tommy rot!

MATTHEW 8: 14–15

> When Peter's wife's ma once fell sick,   781
> A touch from the Lord did the trick.
> He made her so well
> That it cheers me to tell
> She's back at work in half a tick!

You work hard, but work is a pest? 782
You're heavy laden, then the best
Thing you can do – see –
Is to come here with Me.
I tell you that I'll give you rest!

A farmer who scattered some seeds 783
Saw them flourish, despite the weeds.
But he gathered it all
Once the wheat had grown tall.
Sorting bad from good were his deeds!

The tiniest seed in the store 784
Grew enormously large, and more
Than the farmer expected
From seed he'd selected!
God's Kingdom is like that – be sure!

A merchant went looking for pearls – 785
Entranced – just like men fall for girls.
He sold all that he had,
Bought the best pearl, so glad –
In that way God's Kingdom unfurls.

The Kingdom of heaven's a net 786
A fisherman casts out, to get
Enough fish to sell,
Keeping some back as well:
A treat for his friends, and his pet.

A king reckoned up all the debt 787
His servants incurred, and he bet
That if he forgave
Every one, it would pave
The example they also should set!

The manager went out to hire   788
Vineyard workers, in spite of the fire
Of the sun through the day.
When it came to their pay,
Their complaints taught them not to enquire!

MATTHEW 21: 28–31

Two sons were invited to work   789
For their father. One opted to shirk,
While the other said *'Yes.'*
Both changed sides, to impress –
But the *'No'* changed to *'Yes'* won the perk!

MATTHEW 22: 2–14

'Please come to my feast,' said the king,   790
*'The table is set, everything
Is ready for you!'*
But the king really knew
More excuses his guests would soon bring!

MATTHEW 24: 32–33

When fig trees display their nice leaves,   791
You can tell, like wheat stacked in sheaves,
That summer is here,
And the Kingdom is near
When the Jesus disciple believes.

MATTHEW 25: 1–13

Ten girls to the wedding invited,   792
With oil in their lamps well ignited,
The groom came and passed,
But their oil did not last,
Only five of those girls got excited!

MATTHEW 25: 14–30

To servants, a man trusted funds,   793
Gave five, two, and one, of his pounds.
*'Please use them for good,
As you know that you should.
Don't bury your talents – like hounds!'*

Capernaum folk crowded round 794
To be cured by Jesus. One found
The best way for healing
Was down through the ceiling.
'Your sins I forgive! You're unbound!'

'If you find your coat has a tear, 795
And you've nothing else you can wear,
Don't patch up the rent
With new cloth. You are meant
To know new and old just won't pair!'

'If you use an old bottle for wine 796
That is old and mature, then that's fine.
But you really must know
That new wine should not go
Into old ones that don't glint and shine!'

Twelve men Jesus chose for his team, 797
John, Andy, Pip, Pete, and *(Zeb)* Jim,
Nat, Matthew, and Tom,
Jim *(Alph),* Thadd, and Simon,
And Judas, 'cos this was God's scheme!

'If you've got a lamp that's alight, 798
You know that it really is right
To light up the homestead,
Not hide it below bed –
So nothing is hidden from sight!'

Bedevilled, a man they called *'Legion,'* 799
Was healed by Jesus in that region.
The evil went. Fine! –
Entered two thousand swine,
Who drowned in the sea! Owners raging!

A woman, quite poorly, twelve years,   800
Was not getting better, but worse.
She touched His robe's hem –
Jesus felt power stem,
And healed her. She had no more fears!

Jairus, the synagogue's ruler,   801
Had suffered the death of his daughter.
'The lass is not dead,'
Jesus said, *'She's in bed,*
And fast asleep, just as she oughta!'

With her hand in his, Jesus said,   802
'Talitha cumi,' – and then led
Her on to her feet,
And she looked pretty neat –
A twelve year old, passed off as dead!

In synagogue, where Jesus taught,   803
By many, His message was fraught
With taunts. Hear them yell:
'Chippy's son! – you're no swell!'
'But, you *should believe – yes* you ought!'

One birthday, King Herod splashed out   804
By feasting his friends, sparing nowt!
He was so entranced
When Salome veil-danced,
'I'll give you the world, without doubt!'

'You mean it?' she queried, and said   805
'I want John the Baptist's young head
Upon a large plate,
And I'm not going to wait
Forever! Just kill him stone dead!'

King Herod agreed, amidst sadness
That John's head must be hers. What madness!
Disciples soon heard
Of his fate, and interred
John's body. Oh Herod – what badness!

806

MARK 6: 45-52

Jesus, up mountain, alone,
At prayer, sensed his friends might well drown –
The storm was so fierce!
But He said, *'Be at peace –*
It is I!' – and that calmed it all down.

807

MARK 7: 15

'There's nothing that enters within
Which is anything near like sin.
But all that comes out
Is like sin without doubt,
Defiles us, it's true – kith and kin!'

808

MARK 7: 31-37

At Decapolis, a man dumb
And deaf met Jesus who said, *'Come*
Here with me, aside'
Looking up, he then sighed –
'You're healed, Ephphatha! – but stay mum!'

809

MARK 8: 28-29

'Who do men suggest that I am?'
Asked Jesus. *'Elijah? P'haps John?*
A prophet?' 'No way!' –
Blurted Peter – *'I say*
That You ARE The Christ! – yes Sir!' Wham!

810

MARK 9: 2-8

Jesus, with Pete, James, and John,
Alone up the mountain had gone.
A voice from the cloud
Said, to them, right out loud,
'Beloved One – hear Him – My Son!'

811

MARK 10: 13-16

When children were brought for His touch,   812
The disciples complained about such,
But Jesus defied them
With children beside Him,
He loved them, and cared for them much.

MARK 10: 42-45

If you want to be great, Jesus said,   813
And want to be top-dog instead,
You must understand
That the best in the land
Is the servant of all. *He's* the head!

MARK 12: 1-12

'A man had a vineyard he prized,   814
Left servants to tend it. Despised,
Those servants were killed
By the enemy. Willed
His revenge! All the enemy died!'

MARK 14: 43-49

'If you will arrest me, why need   815
You come strongly armed? Yes, indeed
I was teaching each day
In the Temple. No way
Did you seize me!' The Scriptures agreed.

MARK 14: 61-64

'The Christ, are you?' asked the High Priest.   816
'The Son of The Blessed?' he teased.
'I am!' Jesus said.
Caiaphas went quite red –
'For blasphemy – death – at the least!'

LUKE 1: 46-55

'My soul,' Mary said, *'full of joy!*   817
My Saviour, my God – He's my boy!
His mercy's for nations
And all generations,
Forever. For Israel, Le Roi!'

LUKE 1: 68

Blest be Israel's God, the Lord,   818
By David and prophets adored.
Salvation You bring
Because You are our King!
In peace guide our feet on Your road.

LUKE 2: 4

From Nazareth Joseph departed   819
With Mary, and donkey that carted
Them both at a pace
To the Bethlehem place.
But baby, in stable, had started!

LUKE 2: 10-11

To shepherds, at watch by their sheep,   820
The angel brought Good News! *'Don't keep*
It all under cover
But share it: your Saviour
Is born today! Quick – take the Jeep!'

LUKE 2: 25-32

Simeon – righteous, devout –   821
Received the Christ child without doubt.
'Now let me depart
Hence in peace!' From his heart –
'This Light here will never go out!'

LUKE 2: 41-42

We know nothing more of the lad   822
Till twelve years were passed, and he had
A Passover treat
To Jerusalem's seat
In temple, with teachers. Not bad!

LUKE 2: 43-44

His parents were frantic with worry!   823
'No sign of the boy! We must hurry!'
Said Joseph to Mary
'It's really quite scary! –
Where can Jesus be?' Such a flurry!

LUKE 2: 46-49

Three days after – glad to relate,   824
They found him engaged in debate.
'It's my Father's business!'
Said Jesus. *"What is this?'*
Thought Mary, and pondered his fate.

LUKE 2: 51-52

Though neither could quite understand,   825
The three of them went hand in hand
Back to Nazareth town
Where the lad knuckled down
And became the best son in the land.

LUKE 4: 16-29

At Nazareth, as He would do   826
He went to the synagogue. True!
What He read from the books
Brought such terrible looks –
His hearers – they threw Him out! *'Shoo!'*

LUKE 5: 10

'From henceforth, you're going to catch men!'   827
Said Jesus to Peter. *'What then –*
Once fishing is done?'
'You'll catch men by the ton!'
He followed, but thought, *'Starting when?'*

LUKE 9: 1-6

Disciples assembled, He said: 828
'Don't worry yourselves about bread.
You'll not need a thing!
Ditch your luggage! Just bring
Good News to all those where you're led!'

LUKE 9: 23-25

'To those who would follow me there,   829
Your cross, every day, you must bear!
For me, you may die –
Your real life's on high!
What you lose, you will gain! Is that clear?'

'Say – who'll be the greatest? Please tell?'   830
Your Kingdom sounds really quite swell!'
But Jesus looked round,
Saw a child on the ground.
'He's the greatest – this child!' Well, well, well!

'If you're not for me, truly you know   831
It's fact – you're against me! Yes? No?'
This challenged them all,
But they heeded the call:
They were *sure* they were ready to go!

'From Jerus'lem travelled a man   832
To Jericho. Sadly, he ran
Into bandits who mugged him,
Priests came by but shrugged him.
Sole helper – good Samaritan.'

'At midnight a friend rang the bell,   833
And begged for some bread. *"What the hell?"*
Said the sleeper, *"You know*
That it's midnight? E'en so,
A friend must be helped! Very well!"'

'What father, whose child begs for bread   834
Will offer him stones? Those instead,
Or serpents for fish,
Or scorpions a dish,
Not an egg he quite expected?'

'Don't fear idle threats, in a word!   835
God loves you as the smallest bird!
You'll face threat and bluff,
And your lives may be tough!
The price you must pay! Yes – you heard!'

'A farmer's success was the tops,   836
But barns far too small for the crops.
So he built more and bigger
Enhancing his vigour –
But losing his soul in the ops!'

'A vine didn't bear any fruit.   837
The owner decided its root
Should be lifted at once.
But the gardener said, 'Dunce!
Manure it, and then watch it shoot!'

'At weddings, don't choose the best seat.   838
Leave poshest ones for the elite.
Wear humility's gown,
It's the best in the town.
'Till host says, 'Come higher, and eat!'

'A sheep strayed away from the flock,   839
Got lost in the wilderness rock.
The shepherd cared so.
Left the others. 'Let's go
Retrieve it, so no one may mock!'

'A woman's purse fell to the floor,   840
Coins missing – just one, maybe more.
Once down on her knee
She discovered it, see –
Gave neighbours a party till four!'

'A son spent his father's bequest   841
On wine, women, song, and the rest!
Too soon he went broke.
Eating pigs' food, he woke
To a joyful return – a feast!'

'A steward owed pounds to his master.   842
Redeemed his lot very much faster
Being kind to his servants
Reducing their payments,
Commended as wise, not a waster!'

'A rich man had lived it up well.   843
Once dead, he descended to hell.
A poor man who died
Feasted on the far side –
A salutary warning to all!'

'A widow who pesters the judge   844
Can't get his attention to budge.
By keeping on at him
She finally gets him
To take up her case!' Wink, wink, nudge!

'A Pharisee stood up to pray   845
With a flourish, knew what to say.
But a publican slowly
Knelt down, and bowed lowly,
And God hears his prayers to this day!'

Some time Jesus spent, deep in prayer,   846
Disciples he loved were all there.
'O Father, I pray
'Take this cup far away!
Yet, Your will, not mine, I declare!'

Gethsemane, near to the city,   847
Jerusalem's garden, so pretty.
Jesus asked them, 'Please stay
Wide awake while I pray!'
They fell fast asleep. Such a pity!

JOHN 1: 33

John baptised in Jordan's warm water. 848
When Jesus approached, did he oughta?
God's voice heard aloud
Was so plain to the crowd.
His Spirit binds closer than mortar!

JOHN 2: 1–11

In Cana, a wedding was there. 849
Disciples and Jesus did share
The water made wine –
Miraculously fine,
The wedding remarkably rare!

JOHN 3: 16

God so loved the world, yes, that He 850
Gave Jesus, His Son, who would be
The One we will know,
As believers, and go
To be with Him always. You'll see!

JOHN 4: 5–26

A woman Samaritan met 851
At a well, Jesus resting. *'Get*
Living water from me,'
Jesus said. *'Just you see!*
It is I who am speaking! I'm He!'

JOHN 4: 24–26

God *is* Holy Spirit, you see, 852
We worship Him, both One and Three.
Jesus enters the world
With His Kingdom unfurled,
To everyone says, *'I am He!'*

JOHN 5: 1–9

In a pool called Bethesda, they say, 853
Many sick people came day by day.
A cripple in tears,
After thirty long years,
Was restored to good health – *Jesus' way!*

JOHN 6: 1

The crowds followed Jesus all day,   854
Had come with him most of the way.
In a boat, off the coast
A few metres at most,
He taught them what Christians should say!

JOHN 6: 1-14

A crowd had been round Him for hours   855
'They're hungry,' said Jesus. His powers
To feed them He used.
With compassion, He mused –
'Fish and bread, more than ever, are yours!'

JOHN 6: 15-21

One evening as they crossed the sea   856
A storm whipped the waves to frenzy.
'Help, Master, we sink!'
They were right on the brink
Of drowning. Said Jesus: *'Calm be!'*

JOHN 6: 52-59

In synagogue, Jesus decreed   857
'My life is the life you should lead!
Food and drink in my Name
It's my Spirit – the same!
I'm in you, alive as you feed!'

JOHN 8: 51-59

Abraham's nation, the Hebrews   858
Long sought the Messiah. The Jews
In centuries later
Met Jesus, Creator,
Pre-Abraham – yet today's News!

JOHN 9: 1-12

There was a man blind from his birth: 859
A wretched existence on earth.
But Jesus came by
And anointed his eye.
His sight now makes life doubly worth!

JOHN 10: 1-5

A thief, stealing sheep from the fold 860
Has got to make sure that he's bold,
For the shepherd who's true
Watches out for him, so
Beware – sheep know strangers, of old!

JOHN 11: 1-44

Sisters Mary and Martha both cried 861
At Bethany, when Lazarus died,
But Jesus gave orders
'Depart the tomb's borders!'
So when Lazarus heard, he complied!

JOHN 12: 1-8

At supper in Bethany home, 862
Relaxing with Jesus, did come
Mary Magdalene, sweet
Ointment bathing his feet.
Groaned Judas, *'You wastrel, sell some!'*

JOHN 12: 12-16

With Passover time very soon, 863
We know it was nearly full moon.
'A donkey for Master
Will get Him there faster!'
Jerusalem bound, before noon.

JOHN 13: 1-20

The Passover meal had begun 864
When Jesus approached Number One:
'I'll now wash your feet!'
Peter jumped from his seat –
'Wash feet, wash the lot! All in one!'

JOHN 13: 21-30

At supper, the Passover meal, 865
Not sensing how Jesus might feel,
'Just one of you here
Will betray me, I fear!'
'Is it I Lord? Oh please do reveal!'

JOHN 13: 30

'Twas Judas who dipped in the bowl   866
The same time as Jesus. His soul
Bedevilled by Satan.
Remorse quickly set in.
'Betray Him!' – The Sanhedrin's goal.

JOHN 13: 34–35

'A command I give to you now,'   867
Said Jesus, *'A new one, shows how*
To love one another,
But don't hurt each other.
That way, my disciples will grow!'

JOHN 14: 1–6

'Never be worried by fear'   868
Said Jesus, *'Don't fear, with me near!*
I'll prepare your place
In my house. And my face
Will always precede you from here!'

JOHN 14: 16

'Just listen, and learn it from me,   869
I tell you the truth, don't you see –
Once the Comforter's come,
You'll just witness and roam
With the power and the love of JC!'

JOHN 14: 18

'Just love me, and do what I say,'   870
Said Jesus, *'and I'll point the way.*
I'll never forsake you
Nor leave you, but take you
With me on the heavenly way.'

JOHN 14: 25–31

'For yourselves, you'll soon have to fend'   871
Said Jesus, *'but it's not the end.*
Your love and your power
Will grow hour by hour
And the world will eventually bend!'

JOHN 15: 1–11

'Like grapes that you've seen on the vine,
Your life is entwined, yours with mine.
When your roots are healthy,
And harvesting wealthy,
The spiritual fruit is the wine!'

872

JOHN 16: 13

'When the Spirit is come, he'll guide you
To truth, that will soon be inside you.
You'll know what to say
When you're asked on the day!
You'll go with My Presence beside you!'

873

JOHN 16: 28–31

The disciples said, *'It's now plain,*
We never need ask you again!
You came forth from God,
We believe you're The Lord –
It's our job the whole world to gain!'

874

JOHN 18: 12–14

First, Jesus met Annas for trial,
Then Caiaphas, equally vile.
With Passover nigh
One man still had to die –
With or without Peter's denial!

875

JOHN 18: 27

As Peter was at the night Court
Of the High Priest. A maid there thought,
'Jesus' friend – aren't you! Sure!'
Peter cursed and he swore.
Cock crowed the third time, and he wept.

876

JOHN 18: 33–40

Asked Pilate, 'You're *King of the Jews?'*
'You said it,' said Jesus. *'Bad news'*
Thought Pilate, *'I dare not*
Have rivals. I care not –
Let one prisoner die. Crowd, you choose!'

877

They took Jesus out to the cross. 878
His title, *'King of Jews.'* No loss
Felt by Pontius Pilate.
Rage turned red to violet –
The crowd screamed, *'He's never our boss!'*

In Latin, and Hebrew, and Greek – 879
The title of Jesus that week.
Jews looked at the cross
Knowing Pilate was boss.
'What's written is written! I speak!'

For his garments soldiers cast lots, 880
His coat alone must have cost pots!
Then they raised him aloft
On the cross, nails in soft
Flesh. Victim of dastardly plots!

The last words from Jesus' three hours 881
Displayed, even so, divine powers.
'Be mother,' he said,
'Here to son John instead;
And John, behold mother's now yours!'

The soldiers had had a long day. 882
'Dispose of the criminals, yea!
We'll break their legs so
To make sure that they go!'
But Jesus was dead. *'All OK!'*

From Arimathaea, so sad, 883
A councillor, Joseph, who had
A rock tomb nearby
In which Jesus could lie.
When Pilate said *'Yes,'* he was glad.

They bound Jesus' body with spice 884
And buried Him there in a trice.
With Passover near,
They'd a race to get clear.
Set a guard on the tomb. Cold as ice.

To locked Upper Room Mary ran 885
And banged on the door. *'If you can
Believe it,'* – took breath –
*'The Lord's risen from death!
Come look, Peter! John, you'll see, man!'*

Pete reached the tomb well after John. 886
It's true. Jesus' body had gone!
Empty tomb. Body nil!
Yet the grave clothes were still
As they'd left them. Could this be a *con?*

She went to the tomb Sunday morning. 887
The stone was removed, without warning.
She stood back in tears,
'It is I!' Mary hears –
'Your Lord is arisen! No mourning!'

The Upper Room, Monday that week, 888
The doors still locked fast. Not a squeak
The Lord crossed the floor.
*'I'll be with you some more!
Peace be with you!'* he said. Fantastique!

So, Thomas had missed Jesus. *'Shame! –* 889
Must see for myself!' was his claim.
'Just reach out and touch'
Jesus said – *'wounds and such.'*
'My Lord and my God! That's Your Name!'

Days later, his friends went out fishing,   890
And secretly, each of them wishing
That Jesus was risen.
When just past the mizzen,
He stood! *'Be at peace!'* was his greeting.

'Been working all night, with no sight   891
Of a fish?' Jesus said, *'To the right –*
Just cast your nets out!'
One-five-three fish about
Landed up in the hold. What a bite!

A barbecue later that morning   892
Set Peter's true loyalty dawning.
Asked Jesus, *'You love me?'*
'Of course!' *'Reassure me! –*
Feed sheep, lambs, and sheep! Just a warning!'

There are many things Jesus said,   893
And did – words that you have just read.
'If we wrote every one
We'd need books by the ton!
We'd never complete it!' John said.

They sat there in sadness and gloom,   894
When the Spirit roared into the Room.
On fire for their Lord,
They all shouted His Word
In Jerusalem, Rome and Khartoum!

They heard the apostles' strong teaching,   895
They prayed, and they spent the time preaching.
They found that the Word
Which they spread, people heard
In their hundreds! The message was reaching!

ACTS 3: 1–10

When Peter and John were at prayer   896
They saw a man beckon and stare.
'Have you got a few bob?'
Healed him! Right proper job!
'In the name of Lord Jesus, we care!'

ACTS 5: 34–42

Gamaliel, Pharisee there,   897
Wisely urged, *'Apostles we spare!*
If this is of God,
It will pass on the nod!
If not, it will vanish! Thin air!'

ACTS 6: 1–7

Some Grecian widows out there   898
Said mealtimes were simply not fair.
'We're being neglected!'
And so they elected
Sev'n deacons, to give them fair share!

ACTS 7: 54–55

Now Stephen upset all the Jews   899
By fearlessly preaching Good News.
They stoned him to death.
As he took his last breath –
Saw a vision of heaven. Such views!

ACTS 8: 1–3

Saul also was at Stephen's death,   900
Convinced it was God's will on earth:
'All Christians should die!'
He determined, *'Yes I*
Eliminate Christians at birth!'

ACTS 8: 14–17

They laid hands on the entire band   901
And prayed that God's Spirit would land
On all who were true,
So that everyone knew
Lord Jesus, our God, was on hand.

ACTS 8: 26-40

Towards Ethiopia fast   902
A eunuch in chariot passed
Our Philip, who duly
Gave baptism truly.
'Behold, here is water!' At last!

ACTS 9: 1-18

Saul, breathing threatening and slaughter,   903
Killed dad and mum – yes – son and daughter.
On Damascus' road
Jesus called him, aloud!
Became *Paul* – the Christian's aorta!

ACTS 9: 19-22

Ananias was bolder than most,   904
For Saul he became Christian host.
He laid hands on Saul,
Baptised him as Paul,
And helped him receive Holy Ghost.

ACTS 10: 9-13

In Joppa, the sunshine-drenched Peter   905
Dreamed God had plans for him far neater.
'Let all Gentile Jews
Ignore most Jewish views' –
Now Peter, of meat he's an eater!

ACTS 18: 1-7

When first the Good News went abroad,   906
Only Jews thought that they knew the Lord.
Each day it was clear
As the Gentiles got near
They were Christians as well, 'pon my Word.

ACTS 20: 7-12

'Twas Eutychus, young lad, well spoken   907
Who fell asleep, rudely awoken
While Paul preached for hours,
He fell into the flowers
From the window above. Nothing broken!

A storm arose while Paul was sailing 908
His tummy was bilious and ailing.
He prayed more than most,
Got shipwrecked on the coast –
Northeast Malta, with friendship prevailing.

ACTS 28: 30–31

Eventually, Paul reached Rome, 909
And spent two years there, in his home.
He worked making tents,
Preaching Christ to the gents,
Till finally, God called him: *'Come!'*

A note about Romans:
Paul wrote Romans in AD 57.
Romans 13:14 converted Augustine in AD 387,
Romans 1:17 converted Martin Luther in AD 1517
And Luther's preface to Romans converted John
Wesley in AD 1738

This letter to Romans, of Paul – 910
The man who was once known as Saul –
Converted Augustine,
And Luther, and just in
Was Wesley. Remarkable haul!

ROMANS 1: 16–17

The gospel has fantastic power. 911
It enters the soul hour by hour.
The Jews first, then Greeks
Hear the words Spirit speaks,
With the strength of a spiritual tower!

ROMANS 3: 23

We're sinners. We're *all* sinners. Fact. 912
We fall short when we break God's Pact.
Because of God's grace
Yes, the whole human race
Can start again. It's time to act!

ROMANS 5: 8

While we were yet sinners, Christ died   913
For us, but it's hard to decide
What we had done to
Gain His love – we who
Did nothing to be by His side!

ROMANS 6: 1–11

In Baptism, with Christ we die,   914
But rise with him – we tell no lie!
To crucify sin
Means that we aim to win
The lifestyle of Christ. Worth a try!

ROMANS 6: 4

We were buried with Christ in the tomb,   915
Yet His new life broke out of that womb.
If we're dead unto sin
It's His life that we're in
That disperses the old gloom and doom!

ROMANS 8: 22

At present, the world groans in pain,   916
Till Jesus the Christ comes again!
We wait our redemption
And eagerly mention
The spiritual prize we will gain!

ROMANS 8: 35

There's nothing can force us apart   917
With Christ's love so deep in our heart!
Not trouble, or hurry,
Or famine, or worry,
Or peril, or sword, or sin's dart!

ROMANS 8: 38–39

There's nothing God's love cannot beat,   918
Not life, death, in depths, or in height.
Nor angels, nor powers,
Principalities. Ours
Are lives in His hands, till we meet!

ROMANS 10: 13

If *you* state that Jesus is Lord,   919
And mean it – then welcome aboard!
Whoever believes
Will be saved. He receives
Us all. No one's ever ignored!

ROMANS 12: 2

The fashions of this world are such   920
That following them isn't much.
But renew your mind
And you'll very soon find
Transformation comes at the first touch.

ROMANS 12: 4–5

Although we are many, yet we   921
Are Jesus' Body, you see!
His ears, eyes, and mouth,
East and west, north and south,
We're one on this earth! So is He!

ROMANS 13: 13–14

Walk honestly, as in the day.   922
Let each behave decently, yea!
Don't drunkenly revel
Or live like the Devil,
But always proclaim Jesus' way!

ROMANS 14–16

So, whether we live or we die,   923
Please God by example, and try
To live as we should
For we know that it's good
In God's sight! That's all folks – bye bye!

ROMANS 14: 13

The God of hope fill you with joy,   924
And as you believe, peace employ,
That you may abound
In hope, yes, all around –
The power of the Spirit enjoy!

ROMANS 15: 28 (Q.V. ACTS 28: 30–31)

It was Paul's intention – in vain –   925
That one day he might preach in Spain.
But two years in Rome
Proved to be his last home.
Execution his end. What pain!

1 CORINTHIANS 6: 19

Your body needs lots of respect,   926
And doesn't do well by neglect.
As temple-like, fill it
With God's Holy Spirit,
And see that it's frequently checked!

1 CORINTHIANS 11: 23–25

Betrayed, Jesus spoke up, and He   927
Broke bread, and He gave it. *'You'll see –*
My body is this –
And my blood.' (It was His!)
'Just do this in memory of me!'

1 CORINTHIANS 12: 4–11

Want Spiritual gifts to be thine?   928
Or wisdom, or knowledge? That's fine!
Or miracle working
Or prophetic talking,
Discernment, or tongues? It's divine!

1 CORINTHIANS 12: 12–31

The Church is a body, of sorts,   929
With head, hands, heart, feet, even warts!
All parts need to function
Within Spirit's unction,
And share joy or sadness, and thoughts.

1 CORINTHIANS 13

To speak without love, then I am   930
Just hollow. My life is a sham!
When young, I was child-like
But now, I am Christ-like,
With faith, hope, love! Yes Sir! Yes Ma'am!

1 CORINTHIANS 14: 19

In Church, yes, it's better by far:　　　931
Speak five words that so clearly are
Understood by us all –
Where ten thousand appal –
Verbal gobbledygook is a bar!

1 CORINTHIANS 14: 40

If you're going to do anything well,　　　932
You should heed what St. Paul has to tell:
'Let all things you do
Be done decently too,
And in order.' Does that ring a bell?

1 CORINTHIANS 15: 12–22

If Christ never rose from the dead,　　　933
It shouldn't have even been *said!*
The empty tomb's shock
Gave the Jews a real knock –
Made their guards' faces blush rather red!

If Christ did not rise from the dead,　　　934
We might as well pack up, instead!
For Christ's resurrection
Is faith's proclamation,
And Jesus – alive – reigns: our Head!

2 CORINTHIANS 3: 6

We know good laws need to be made,　　　935
Agree that they should be obeyed.
But the Spirit gives life
Where the law just brings strife,
The more so, when it's been man-made!

2 CORINTHIANS 9: 7

If you give God some of your money　　　936
For His Church's work, it's not funny
To grudgingly spare
What you grudgingly share.
Give cheerfully! Be bright and sunny!

2 CORINTHIANS 11: 16–31

The greatest apostle, once *'Saul,'*　937
Lists beatings, and shipwrecks, and all,
With hunger and thirst.
What placed him *the first*
Was his weakness – which made him *Saint Paul!*

2 CORINTHIANS 13: 14

The grace of Christ Jesus our Lord,　938
The love of God – all this is stored,
The fellowship too
Of His Spirit, with you!
Three in One! God forever adored!

GALATIANS 3: 28

You might be a Greek, or a Jew,　939
Or female or male, but it's true
Whether servant or free
We are *one* – don't you see –
One in Christ! That means *us! I and you!*

GALATIANS 5: 22–23

The fruit of the Spirit's for you:　940
Love, joy, peace – they're Spirit-fruit too!
Longsuffering, kindness,
Goodness, and faithfulness,
Meekness, and temperance. True!

GALATIANS 6: 10

While we have the time, let us do　941
Good to all men, 'specially to
All those who belong
To faith's household, so strong –
As well as to others, like you!

EPHESIANS 4: 15

If we fight, or we argue, or moan,　942
Or we criticise harshly, or groan,
There is one thing to know:
Yes! Wherever we go
Speak in love! – Our spiritual phone!

EPHESIANS 6: 10–18

Put on the whole armour of God.   943
Our fight is against flesh and blood.
It means we will stand
In the evil day, and
Defeat wicked powers as we should!

EPHESIANS 6: 10–18

Stand therefore, with truth round your frame   944
And righteousness' breastplate, the same.
Your feet shod with peace
Deflect darts, as if grease,
And helmet and sword? – Spirit's flame!

PHILIPPIANS 2: 5–10

Be careful to see that your mind   945
Is just as in Jesus you find.
He served us, so humble.
The Cross makes folk stumble.
Accept God's instructions, defined!

PHILIPPIANS 4: 7

The peace that I give you, of God –   946
Past all understanding. A rod
And staff there to guide you,
A haven to hide you.
Christ's way, hearts and minds will have trod.

PHILIPPIANS 4: 11–12

I try to be fairly content.   947
Things go wrong – like things that are meant
To go right, but they don't.
It's a test when they won't.
But with Jesus, it's all heaven-sent!

COLOSSIANS 1: 9

We pray for you all, every day,   948
And want you to know why we say:
'Fill up to the brim
With the knowledge of Him!' –
Be wise in the spiritual way!

COLOSSIANS 3: 16

When Jesus speaks deep in your thought,   949
You'll teach and behave as you ought,
Sing psalms all day long,
Hymns and spiritual song –
It's *God's* grace, and cannot be bought!

COLOSSIANS 3: 18–23

Be gentle and kind in your life,   950
It's better to love! There's no strife
Where family and friends
Really *do* make amends –
That's children, and husband, and wife!

COLOSSIANS 3: 23–24

Whatever you think, say, or do,   951
Just do it for Jesus! And you
Will get your reward –
Not from men – but The Lord!
You know this is right! Yes – it's true!

1 THESSALONIANS 4: 14–18

We long to be one with The Lord,   952
For this is His promise, His word:
At the trumpet blast sound,
When the voice shouts around –
Caught up in the air – *'Come aboard!'*

1 THESSALONIANS 5: 1–6

We don't know the time or the place   953
To meet Jesus Christ face to face.
We need to be ready
And sober and steady,
And watchful. On guard – just in case!

1 THESSALONIANS 5: 12–18

Encouragement! This is the clue   954
To build up the fellowship. True!
Look after the weak,
And keep order, and speak
Peace, and joy. Pray now. God loves *you!*

When things go so terribly wrong,   955
It's hard for you to get along –
Just trust in the Lord
And take Him at His word!
'The Lord is our Saviour!' – our song!

1 TIMOTHY 1: 15

This is a true saying, you know,   956
And worth of note, as you go:
Christ Jesus came here
To save sinners, my dear,
Of whom I'm the chief. There you go!

1 TIMOTHY 5: 18

Let ox without muzzle grind corn.   957
Pay workers their dues night and morn.
To do the Lord's work
Is the worthiest perk.
To teach may be why you were born!

1 TIMOTHY 5: 23

Young Timothy, Bishop much later   958
Of Ephesus, used to sip water.
'Drink wine for the sake
Of your tummy, and make
Life purer!' was now what Paul taught. Ah!

2 TIMOTHY 1 & 2

I pray that the gift which God gave you   959
Develops and grows. Let it save you!
Your faith will grow strong
As you journey along!
Hold fast to my teachings, I pray you!

2 TIMOTHY 4: 7–8

I fought the good fight to the end!   960
I finished the course. I'll not bend
From the doctrine of Christ.
I'll back Him to the last!
A righteousness crown He will send!

2 TIMOTHY 4: 11–13

Dear Luke is the only one with me.   961
Take Mark, and bring him, as well, with thee.
Find parchment and books
And my cloak on the hooks
Left with Carpus, at Troas – my dear T!

TITUS 1: 7

It's very important to know   962
How Christian people should go:
No brawling or striking!
And don't get a liking
For lucre so filthy! No, no!

TITUS 1: 8

A bishop should set an example   963
And really be Christlike. A sample:
Be sober, and you should
Be temperate, and good
And faithful. Encourage your people!

PHILEMON

A slave who has left you in haste?   964
Invite him to come back. Don't waste
The chance to make up,
Without punishment. Sup
Together as friends now! Act fast!

HEBREWS 1

Whoever penned 'Hebrews,' he wrote   965
Encouraging Christians to note
That things will get better!
Please search through this letter!
'Best literary Greek!' – they quote!

HEBREWS 2

It speaks of Christ Jesus the man   966
Above all the angels. How can
We fail to adore him
And trust him? Our anthem
In rough times – He'll not let us down!

HEBREWS 10: 4

To take away sins, it was thought
That animal sacrifice sought
Forgiveness divine
Of the wrongs – yours and mine.
Atonement can never be bought!

967

HEBREWS 10: 25

It's easy to think we don't need
To meet up together. But we'd
Do better to meet
Far more often, and greet:
Encourage each other! *Indeed!*

968

HEBREWS 11

By faith, men of old lived their lives.
By faith, so we read, did their wives.
The lesson we learn
Is so plain. We discern
Their faith was as sharp as sharp knives!

969

HEBREWS 12: 1–2

With witnesses clouding around
We're urged not to let sin abound,
But patiently run
Now the race has begun,
With Jesus, who's at God's right hand!

970

HEBREWS 13: 5

Don't get an obsession for money,
Like bees that are dazzled by honey.
Remember the teaching
Of Jesus, His preaching:
'You can't take it with you!' That's funny!

971

HEBREWS 13: 8

There's one thing that time will not sever:
Our Jesus – the same, now and ever.
He'll always be here,
And He'll bring us good cheer!
He'll never forsake us! That's *never!*

972

The Shepherd of all faithful sheep,   973
The God of all peace – He will keep
Our hearts and our minds
In perfection. He binds
Us all in one flock. A clean sweep!

JAMES 2: 22–27

It's something we've all got to do –   974
Be doers, not just hearers, who
Hear all that is said
But delude ourselves! Dead
Religion is vain! Yes – it's true!

JAMES 5: 14

Is any among you not well?   975
It's better for us if you tell
The Church, who will pray
With you all, day by day.
Anointing and healing. That's swell!

1 PETER 1: 3

Blessed be the God and Father –   976
Jesus Christ, our Lord, I gather,
Made us born again
Into hope – that was when
He rose from the dead. Yes Sir! Rather!

1 PETER 2: 1

Dump wickedness into the bin!   977
Hypocrisy, guile – they're all sin!
To envy is wrong,
Or speak evil. Be strong!
And *that* way, the Devil won't win!

1 PETER 2: 7

The stone which the builders rejected   978
Is cornerstone safely erected!
It's *Jesus* we mean,
And it's plain to be seen
That in Jesus our life is perfected!

1 PETER 3: 8

Like-minded, compassionate – you
Must be tender-hearted, you too!
In humbleness live,
And for evil don't give
Evil back! That's *blessing!* It's true!

979

1 PETER 5: 8

Be sober, be vigilant, while
Your enemy – devilish guile,
With a lion's great roar
He devours all the poor
In his way! Whom resist every mile!

980

1 PETER 5: 10

It's God who has called you in grace.
In suffering, Christ takes first place.
He's first in your life.
He'll perfect you in strife
As he strengthens you all, face to face.

981

2 PETER

Possibly it's the last letter
Written in the NT. Better
To see it construed
As a re-write of Jude,
Used by 2 Peter as a trend-setter!

982

1 JOHN 1: 8–9

If we say we're not sinners, then
We know we deceive ourselves when
That's not true. Confess
And repent, more or less –
And God will forgive you, I ken!

983

1 JOHN 2: 1–2

If any man sin, we have found
In Jesus, an Advocate sound.
He mediates now
Though we need not ask how –
We know we're forgiven all round!

984

1 JOHN 3: 2

The children of God now are we,   985
We don't know quite how, but we'll see
Our Lord as he is
And be like him – be His!
The promise from our Lord, JC!

1 JOHN 3: 18

To love someone, love has to be   986
Done, not just *said* – now do you see!
In deed and in truth
In old age and in youth –
Commands for us all – 1 John 3.

1 JOHN 4: 18

Now, perfect love casts out all fear!   987
It's true, and we know year by year:
Whoever receives this
Will always believe this!
Love God, for He's always so near!

2 JOHN

The second Epistle of John   988
In thirteen short verses – it's gone!
The message we get
Is of love – love and yet
It needs to be said – on and on!

3 JOHN

3 John is as short. One verse more   989
Than 2 John, and yet he still saw
That Christians do better
Despite his short letter
Providing they value verse 4!

JUDE

This letter, to Christians all over   990
The world – though at first, Asia Minor –
Encourages all
To rise up, when we fall,
And shelter beneath Spirit's cover!

REVELATION 1: 8-9

> 'True: Alpha and Omega, I'm 991
> The first, and the last, and the same.
> I promise to be
> Here for you, don't you see –
> I was, and will be, and I AM.'

REVELATION 1: 11

To Asian Churches wrote John, 992
Ephesus, Smyrna, Pergamum,
Thyatira and Sardis,
Philadelphia – oh yes –
And Laodicaea! All done!

REVELATION 3: 14-16

In Laodicaea, the form 993
Of Christians was only lukewarm!
'Be one or the other
My dear Christian brother!
Not cold, warm, but hot! That's the norm!'

REVELATION 4

The vision of heaven was one 994
Surrounded by jewels. A throne,
Twenty elders, creatures
With fantastic features –
Prostrated, in worship begun.

REVELATION 4-6

In secret, the Christians met there. 995
Symbolic, the language they share.
Such as, 'Lamb,' 'scrolls,' and 'seals,'
'Angels,' 'creatures,' and 'wheels:'
All revealed – to the reader aware!

REVELATION 7

The servants of God bore a mark 996
On foreheads, spiritual spark
Which set them apart
Setting fire to the heart
Lighting 144-three-0s in dark.

The angel's sound – yes, number seven   997
Was followed by voices in heaven.
Then worship took place
Amidst thunder apace,
And opened God's temple for all men.

REVELATION 13

The Emperor, Roman Domitian   998
Was expert at number addition.
His dastardly tricks
Totalled six-sixty-six.
He's Antichrist, Beast. Evil mission!

REVELATION 16

God's angels cast wrath on the earth.   999
'Death's better for men than their birth!'
His angels poured bowl
After bowl on the whole
Of the wickedness there. It was dearth!

REVELATION 21

'Come here. I will show you the things   1000
To follow!' said angel with wings.
'New heaven and earth,
New Jerusalem's birth!
No tears! No more dying!' – he sings.

REVELATION 22

The Apostle John, he gave cheer   1001
And finally wrote without fear.
'After suffering and pain
We'll see Jesus again!
Come Jesus, come Jesus! We're here!'

Author's epilogue

The Bible Word never retires.
Read now, while the Spirit inspires.
Find out that it's true!
What does God say to *you?*
Then do it, until breath expires!

About this book

After seeing "The New Testament In Limerick Verse" – many people suggested that the Old Testament and The Apocrypha should also be published in the same sort of format.

What is contained in this book, therefore, is by no means perfect, but it does attempt to include the major themes and personalities of the Old Testament, and The Apocrypha.

It has the same aim – to encourage people to read the real thing. If not – and if this is the only work that people ever read – then at least they will have gleaned a flavour of what the Bible is about.

I can visualise people waiting in hotels or aiport lounges for a connexion in about three hours' time, having nothing to occupy their minds. If they were to see this book, I reckon that they would read it very easily – from cover to cover!

I can see it being really helpful to teachers, faced with a fourth –year class taking RE as the last period on a Friday afternoon in the heat of summer.

I can envisage it lying around in doctors' and dentists' waiting rooms.

This book could be of enormous help to clergy, in Confirmation preparation, or to people who have shied away from church, simply because some worship seems to be so dauntingly complicated and wordy.

The good thing about it is that much of The Old Testament provided the Scriptures which helped to form the mind of Jesus. And, as St. Paul said, *"Have this mind be in you, which was also In Christ Jesus!" (Phil.2:5)* – and this is the motivation behind the work.

Yes – I know that some of the rhymes have been stretched to the limits, and that it has been necessary occasionally to áccent a syllable, in order that it should be easier to make the rhythm fit better – but, as nobody has ever done this exercise before, then hopefully it's better than nothing!

I hope *do* hope that it encourages you to read *the real thing*!

Christopher Goodwins
Isleham
26 April 2006

O

is a symbol of the world,
of oneness and unity. O Books
explores the many paths of whole-
ness and spiritual understanding which
different traditions have developed down
the ages. It aims to bring this knowledge in
accessible form, to a general readership, providing practical spirituality to today's seekers.

For the full list of over 200 titles covering:
ACADEMIC/THEOLOGY • ANGELS • ASTROLOGY/
NUMEROLOGY • BIOGRAPHY/AUTOBIOGRAPHY
• BUDDHISM/ENLIGHTENMENT • BUSINESS/LEADERSHIP/
WISDOM • CELTIC/DRUID/PAGAN • CHANNELLING
• CHRISTIANITY; EARLY • CHRISTIANITY; TRADITIONAL
• CHRISTIANITY; PROGRESSIVE • CHRISTIANITY;
DEVOTIONAL • CHILDREN'S SPIRITUALITY • CHILDREN'S
BIBLE STORIES • CHILDREN'S BOARD/NOVELTY • CREATIVE
SPIRITUALITY • CURRENT AFFAIRS/RELIGIOUS • ECONOMY/
POLITICS/SUSTAINABILITY • ENVIRONMENT/EARTH
• FICTION • GODDESS/FEMININE • HEALTH/FITNESS
• HEALING/REIKI • HINDUISM/ADVAITA/VEDANTA
• HISTORY/ARCHAEOLOGY • HOLISTIC SPIRITUALITY
• INTERFAITH/ECUMENICAL • ISLAM/SUFISM
• JUDAISM/CHRISTIANITY • MEDITATION/PRAYER
• MYSTERY/PARANORMAL • MYSTICISM • MYTHS
• POETRY • RELATIONSHIPS/LOVE • RELIGION/
PHILOSOPHY • SCHOOL TITLES • SCIENCE/
RELIGION • SELF-HELP/PSYCHOLOGY
• SPIRITUAL SEARCH • WORLD
RELIGIONS/SCRIPTURES • YOGA

**Please visit our website,
www.O-books.net**